TORONTO

TRAVEL GUIDE

Essential Information and Tips to Prepare for Your Trip: Everything You Should Know Before You Go

Kemp Z. Todd

TABLE OF CONTENTS

IMPORTANT NOTE:

This travel guide is designed to provide you with comprehensive, practical, and engaging information about your destination. However, it is important to note that this guide does not include images, maps, or other visual aids. Instead, we have focused on delivering detailed descriptions, helpful tips, and valuable insights to enhance your travel experience.

The absence of images and maps is intentional to ensure the content remains original, high-quality, and straightforward. We encourage you to use this guide alongside reliable maps, navigation tools, and trusted websites for visual references when planning your trip.

While every effort has been made to provide accurate and up-to-date information, travel conditions, attractions, and other details may change over time. We recommend double-checking important details, such as addresses, prices, and operating hours, before making any travel arrangements.

This guide aims to inspire, inform, and assist you in crafting memorable experiences at your destination. We hope you find the content valuable and enjoyable as you explore all the fantastic places awaiting you.

Happy travels!

SCAN CODE TO VIEW
MAP OF TORONTO

Chapter 1: Introduction to Toronto

Welcome to Toronto, a city where skyscrapers meet lake views and every street tells a different story. On my first visit, I stepped off the plane at Billy Bishop Airport and felt the buzz right away—commuters on the streetcar, cyclists weaving through traffic, and a mix of languages floating through the air. That moment set the tone for my week here: a place where you can wander into a quiet garden, then minutes later be surrounded by street art in a lively market. Known for its friendly vibe and safe streets, Toronto welcomes visitors from all walks of life. This guide will help you dive into Toronto's energy and find your own moments of surprise.

In this guide, you'll get honest tips on how to move around—like why I love topping up a Presto card at the subway station, then hopping on a streetcar to reach Kensington Market. There, I found the best taco stand by following a friendly vendor's advice, and I ended up chatting with locals over a cold drink on a sunny afternoon. Practical tips like wearing comfortable shoes and checking the weather forecast before you head out can save you from sore feet and unexpected rain. Toronto's seasons change fast, so packing layers and a small umbrella is smart.

Food in Toronto reflects its people. At St. Lawrence Market, I sampled peameal bacon on a bun while talking to the butcher who told me stories of his family's market stall. On other days, I chased down dim sum in Chinatown or tried butter chicken in Little India. This guide will point you to the spots that locals swear by, from hidden food trucks to family-run diners. I'll share tips on how to avoid long lines—like arriving before peak lunch hour or downloading apps to reserve a table. Your taste buds will thank you.

Beyond the city's towers, green spaces offer a quick break. One afternoon, I packed sandwiches and rode the ferry to the Toronto Islands. I spent hours biking along the trails, watched kids play at the beach, and enjoyed skyline views across the water. Back in the city, High Park's cherry blossoms in spring feel like a secret show—locals spread blankets on the grass, and I joined in, sharing snacks with new friends. I'll tell you when to catch each park at its best and which paths are wheelchair friendly or great for families with strollers.

But Toronto is not just its famous sights. I wandered into Graffiti Alley one evening and found walls covered in art that changed my view of the city. I'll show you where to look for street murals, cozy bookstores, and quiet corners in busy neighborhoods. You don't need to follow a strict plan—some of the best finds happen when you let yourself get a little lost. I'll give you simple steps for offline maps, share the best apps to spot local events, and remind you to pause and enjoy the small moments that make travel real. And remember to carry a refillable water bottle to stay hydrated while you wander.

By the end of this guide, you'll feel ready to explore Toronto with confidence. You'll have routes for your first subway ride, a list of must-see markets, and tips for fitting in like a local. Whether you have one day or one week, this book offers clear plans and space for you to add your own discoveries. I'll also include tips for staying on budget and suggestions for hidden gems in each neighborhood. Toronto is a city that rewards curiosity, and I can't wait for you to find the spots that speak to you. Let's get started and uncover the Toronto that waits beyond the guidebooks.

Why Visit Toronto?

Toronto is a city of surprises. At first glance, you see a modern skyline framed by the CN Tower, glass-fronted condos, and busy streets. But dig a little deeper, and you'll find leafy parks, hidden alleys, and friendly neighborhoods where local life feels both relaxed and vibrant. Whether you're chasing big-city thrills or quiet moments by the lake, Toronto delivers.

First, the landmarks. The CN Tower still tops most bucket lists—you can ride its glass elevator up 1,136 feet for a view that stretches over Lake Ontario. If heights aren't your thing, the tower's EdgeWalk lets thrill-seekers circle the roof on a harness. Nearby, the Royal Ontario Museum and Art Gallery of Ontario house world-class collections. On a rainy afternoon, these museums offer a perfect refuge.

Next, the neighborhoods. Stroll the cobblestone streets of the Distillery District, where Victorian industrial buildings host artisan shops, galleries, and cafés. Wander into Kensington Market to find vintage clothing stores, street art, and Caribbean jerk chicken stands side by side. Head east to Leslieville for a quieter, family-friendly vibe—bakeries and brunch spots spill onto patios in good weather. Each pocket of the city has its own feel, so carve out time to explore beyond downtown.

Toronto's food scene alone is reason enough to visit. You can start the day with South Indian dosas in Little India, grab Chinese dim sum in downtown's Chinatown, then catch an Italian espresso in Corso Italia. St. Lawrence Market, a two-floor hall of fresh produce and local specialties, is perfect for sampling. Don't miss peameal bacon sandwiches at Carousel Bakery or local craft beers at nearby breweries. Street food trucks pop up around the city, especially at lunchtime—look for poutine topped with pulled pork or falafel wraps.

All year round, there's a festival or event to join. In September, TIFF (Toronto International Film Festival) draws movie stars and fans from around the globe. Summer brings Caribana, North America's largest Caribbean carnival, with colorful parades and steel-pan music. Nuit Blanche, a free all-night art festival in October, lights up the city with interactive installations. Even winter has its charms: Winterlicious features prix-fixe menus at top restaurants, and skating on the Natrel Rink under the city lights is a local tradition.

Practical tip: if you plan to hit several major attractions, consider the Toronto CityPASS. It bundles admission to five top sites at a discount and lets you skip some ticket lines. Toronto is busiest in July and August, so if you prefer smaller crowds, aim for May–June or September–October. Even in winter, days around New Year's bring festive markets without the summer rush.

The Spirit of the Six: What Makes Toronto Unique

When you hear locals call their city "the Six," they're referring to the six municipalities—Old Toronto, Scarborough, Etobicoke, York, East York, and North York—that merged in 1998. But "the Six" has grown into more than an administrative label. It's a badge of local pride, a shorthand for Toronto's blend of distinct communities that form a single, dynamic city.

At its heart, the Spirit of the Six is about unity in diversity. Walk along Yonge Street, and you'll pass a Latin American bakery, a South Asian grocery, and a Somali café within blocks. Each community brings its own festivals, food, and traditions, yet they blend seamlessly into the city's daily rhythm. During Caribana, for example, Scarborough's West Indian community leads a parade through downtown, and residents from across the city line the streets in costume and song.

Sports also capture that spirit. Whether cheering for the Maple Leafs, Raptors, or Blue Jays, Torontonians across boroughs unite under one banner. On game nights, bars fill with fans in team jerseys, strangers high-five as soon as a big play happens, and the city feels like one giant living room. Even when teams lose, the shared experience strengthens bonds among residents.

Public transit is another place you'll sense the Six in action. The TTC's subway lines, buses, and streetcars link neighborhoods that feel worlds apart. On a morning commute, you might overhear Mandarin, Punjabi, and Arabic as fellow riders chat. Someone might point a visitor to the nearest subway entrance; another might help you load your Presto card. That everyday kindness—part practical, part welcoming—is the Spirit of the Six in motion.

Artists and entrepreneurs capture the Six in their work. Street art in Graffiti Alley tells stories of local heroes, while indie designers in Queen West blend cultural motifs into fashion and jewelry. Community centers host workshops on everything from Caribbean drumming to Polish paper cutting, open to all who want to learn. When you buy from a family-run café in Little Italy or an artisanal shop in Roncesvalles, you're supporting a neighborhood's unique character.

Even the city's green spaces reflect this unity. High Park's cherry blossoms draw crowds from across Toronto each spring; people picnic side by side under pink blooms. The Toronto Islands, just a short ferry ride away, serve as a communal backyard—families bike its trails, couples picnic by the beach, and friends gather for barbecues. Here, you feel the Six as a shared playground rather than six separate zones.

Practical advice: to tap into the Spirit of the Six, don't just stick to downtown. Take a day to ride the subway or streetcar to Scarborough's Bluffs or Etobicoke's Humber Bay Park. Chat with shop owners, ask for neighborhood tips, and attend a local event.

Diversity and Multiculturalism in Everyday Life

Toronto's claim to fame is its multicultural makeup: nearly half the population was born outside Canada, and more than 200 ethnic groups call the city home. This diversity shapes everything you see, taste, and experience. Rather than siloed enclaves,

Toronto's cultural communities flow into each other, creating neighborhoods that are both distinct and interconnected.

Start with food—perhaps the clearest sign of Toronto's global reach. In the same day, you can feast on Caribbean roti in Eglinton West, Korean bibimbap in North York, and Mexican tacos in Parkdale. Food trucks line King Street West at lunchtime, offering everything from vegan samosas to Japanese-style hot dogs. Pop-up night markets spring up in parking lots, showcasing street food from around the world. Each bite tells a story of migration, adaptation, and shared passion for good food.

Beyond cuisine, you'll find cultural events year-round. Taste of the Danforth celebrates Greek food and music in August; the Chinatown Festival honors Chinese heritage in the summer; and the Toronto Ukrainian Festival in July brings folk dance and borscht to Bloor Street. These festivals are open to all, and they transform city streets into open-air community halls. You don't need a background in these cultures to join in—just an appetite for exploration

Everyday services reflect this blend, too. Signage in subway stations often includes multiple languages. In hospitals and community centers, translation services are common. You might hear announcements in French, Mandarin, or Punjabi on the TTC. Local libraries offer free language classes and host story hours in different tongues. This accessibility makes Toronto welcoming, especially for first-time visitors navigating a new city.

Even Toronto's workplaces and universities mirror this mix. Corporate offices might have staff meetings where colleagues greet each other in half a dozen languages. On campus, student clubs celebrate heritage months—Black History Month, Diwali, Lunar New Year—with performances, food stalls, and workshops open to the public. These events are a low-pressure way to learn and connect.

Practical tip: to experience this diversity up close, visit St. Lawrence Market on a weekday morning. Stallholders come from dozens of countries, and many love to chat about their specialties. Ask about the origins of their cheeses or the best way to prepare a spice blend. For a deeper dive, join a small-group food tour—local guides will take you to hidden gems in different neighborhoods and share personal stories.

Language, Currency, and Local Customs

Toronto is primarily English-speaking, but the city's soundscape is a chorus of languages. You'll hear Cantonese, Tagalog, Punjabi, Arabic, and more on sidewalks, in shops, and aboard the TTC. Most locals are happy to switch to English for visitors, but learning a simple greeting—"Ni hao" in Chinatown or "Shukriya" in Little India—can spark a smile and a helpful tip.

Money in Toronto is in Canadian dollars (CAD). Coins include 5¢ (nickel), 10¢ (dime), 25¢ (quarter), $1 (loonie), and $2 (toonie). Bills come in $5, $10, $20, $50, and $100. ATMs are everywhere, and most accept international cards with a small fee. Credit cards are widely used, even for small purchases, but it's good to carry some cash for street food or market stalls.

Tipping is part of the local culture. In restaurants, aim for 15–20% of the pre-tax bill. Bartenders expect $1–2 per drink. For taxis and rideshares, 10–15% is standard. Hotel porters and housekeeping staff appreciate $1–2 per bag or per night. If you're unsure, check your receipt—many restaurants now include a suggested tip line.

Toronto's locals value politeness and personal space. Hold doors for people entering behind you. Wait for pedestrians to clear before stepping into the street. On transit, offer seats to seniors, pregnant people, or those with mobility aids. Small gestures go a long way and reflect the city's welcoming nature.

Jaywalking—crossing mid-block or against the light—is common, but not without risk. Toronto drivers expect you to obey signals, so use crosswalks and wait for the walk sign. Cycling rules are similar—stick to bike lanes, signal turns, and wear a helmet if you can. The city enforces traffic laws strictly, especially around schools and parks.

If you're invited into someone's home, remove your shoes at the door—most families keep indoor footwear off carpets. Bringing a small gift—wine, chocolates, or a souvenir from your home country—is a nice touch. At social gatherings, hosts may offer food and drinks; it's polite to accept at least a small portion.

Public restrooms are generally free in malls, libraries, and major attractions. In cafés, look for signs or ask staff. Many restaurants reserve restrooms for customers, so a quick coffee or small purchase is a courteous way to gain access.

Finally, Toronto runs on a friendly efficiency. You'll find recycling bins next to garbage cans—separate paper, plastics, and compost. Queues move quickly, and people generally respect personal space. When in doubt, smile, say "sorry" if you bump into someone, and carry on. These small customs help keep the city running smoothly and make your trip more comfortable.

Safety, Cleanliness, and Traveler Friendliness

Toronto consistently ranks among the safest large cities in North America. Violent crime is low in tourist areas, though petty theft—pickpockets or bike-theft—can occur in crowded spots. Keep your valuables secure: use a money belt or keep your phone and wallet in front pockets. If you're cycling, invest in a sturdy lock.

Streets and public spaces are well-maintained. Sidewalks are swept regularly, parks are mowed and watered, and public washrooms are cleaned throughout the day. You'll find recycling and trash bins on almost every block—helping the city stay clean. When you see trash or recycling bins, use them; it's a small step that locals appreciate.

Toronto's police force is visible but low-key. Officers on foot or bike patrol busy districts; you can approach them with questions or concerns. Emergency services respond quickly—dial 911 for police, fire, or medical emergencies. Non-urgent help is available at local community centers or by calling 311 for city services.

Public transit safety is good at all hours. Subways and streetcars run until around 1 AM on weekdays and later on weekends. Platforms have emergency phones and well-lit waiting areas. If you ever feel uneasy, move to a busier car or sit near the operator's booth. Many riders travel late after concerts or sporting events without issue.

Women traveling alone report feeling safe in most parts of the city, even at night. Stick to well-lit streets and main thoroughfares after dark. Avoid isolated parks or alleyways, especially if you're unfamiliar with the area. Ride-hailing apps like Uber or Lyft are reliable late at night; check the license plate and driver details before you get in.

Toronto's health system is high quality. Pharmacies are open late and staff can recommend over-the-counter remedies. If you need medical care, walk-in clinics handle minor injuries and illnesses; hospitals treat emergencies. Travel insurance with health coverage is wise—while care is excellent, costs can be high for visitors.

Anecdote: I once dropped my wallet on a busy streetcar. Moments later, a fellow passenger tapped my shoulder and handed it back—intact. That quick act of honesty reflects how many Torontonians treat strangers: with respect and consideration.

Finally, Toronto's city staff and volunteers go out of their way to help. Look for tourist information booths at Union Station and major attractions. Volunteers at festivals wear bright vests and carry maps. If you get lost, ask a shopkeeper or barista—they'll often draw you a quick map or point you down the right street.

Essential Apps and Services (Presto, TTC, Uber, Weather)

Navigating Toronto is easier when you have the right apps and services at your fingertips. Here are the essentials to download before you arrive—or as soon as you land.

Presto
Presto is a reloadable smart card you use on the TTC (subways, buses, streetcars), GO Transit, and some municipal services. You can buy and top up Presto cards online, at subway stations, or at select retailers. Tap on and off at each ride—fares are deducted automatically, and transfers are free within two hours. A daily fare cap ensures you never pay more than the cost of two single rides in one day.

TTC (Toronto Transit Commission)
The TTC app shows real-time schedules for subways, streetcars, and buses. It maps routes, estimates arrival times, and alerts you to service changes. Use it to plan your trip—enter your start and end points, and the app suggests the fastest route, whether by subway, streetcar, or bus. Remember, subway lines run roughly every 2–5 minutes during peak times and every 7–10 minutes off-peak. Streetcars and buses can be slower in rush hour traffic, so build in extra time if you have tight connections.

Uber / Lyft / Local Taxis
While public transit covers most areas, rideshares fill the gaps—late at night, during bad weather, or for neighborhoods with less frequent service. Uber and Lyft are widely used; fares surge during rush hour or large events, so check prices before you book. For a more local touch, download the Beck Taxi or Royal Taxi apps—these connect you to licensed city cabs.

Bike Share (Bike Share Toronto)

If you prefer two wheels, Bike Share Toronto has stations across the downtown core and beyond. Purchase a single trip, day pass, or monthly membership in the app. Bikes are sturdy and comfortable, with three gears—perfect for gentle hills. Return your bike to any station; late fees apply if you keep it longer than 30 minutes per ride.

Weather Apps

Toronto's weather changes fast. A sunny morning can turn into a rainy afternoon. Apps like The Weather Network or Environment Canada give hour-by-hour forecasts and weather alerts. Check before you head out, and keep a small umbrella or light rain jacket in your bag. In winter, look for ice warnings—sidewalks and streets can get slick, especially near the lake.

City Apps and Info

- **311 Toronto**: Report potholes, graffiti, or noise complaints. You can also use it to find city service information.

- **TO GraffitiTO**: Maps street art locations across the city—great for self-guided mural tours.

- **Fresh City Farms**: Order local produce and groceries for delivery or pickup—handy if you're staying in an apartment.

Event & Dining Apps

- **Eventbrite**: Browse local events, workshops, and small concerts.

- **OpenTable**: Reserve tables at popular restaurants—Toronto's best spots fill up fast, especially on weekends.

Quick Facts: Geography, Layout, and Neighborhoods

Toronto sits on the north shore of Lake Ontario, stretching about 50 km east to west and 25 km north to south. The city is organized in a rough grid downtown, with streets running north–south (numbered or lettered) and avenues running east–west (named after British royalty or local landmarks). Beyond the core, highways and arterial roads link diverse neighborhoods.

Downtown Core

- **Financial District**: Glass towers, business crowds, Union Station.
- **Entertainment District**: Scotiabank Arena, TIFF Bell Lightbox, theatres.
- **Harbourfront**: Waterfront trails, parks, ferry docks to the Toronto Islands.

Central Neighborhoods

- **Kensington Market**: Tight alleys, colorful shops, global eats.
- **Chinatown**: Asian groceries, herbal shops, dim sum restaurants.
- **Queen West**: Trendy boutiques, street art, indie galleries.
- **Yorkville**: Upscale shops, art galleries, fine dining.

East End

- **The Beaches**: Sand beaches, boardwalk, laid-back cafes.
- **Leslieville**: Family-friendly, brunch spots, vintage shops.
- **Danforth (Greektown)**: Greek restaurants, festivals, bakeries.

West End

- **Parkdale**: Eclectic mix, new restaurants, art studios.
- **Roncesvalles**: Polish bakeries, cafes, community parks.
- **High Park**: Large green space, zoo, cherry blossoms in spring.

North of Downtown

- **York**: Residential pockets, community centers, strip malls.
- **East York**: Quiet streets, local shops, small-town feel.
- **Scarborough**: Bluffs, parks, diverse dining.
- **North York**: High-rise condos, shopping malls, cultural centers.

Getting around is easiest by focusing on one or two areas per day. Downtown and the central neighborhoods are walkable, but if you venture farther, the subway and streetcar network covers most main corridors. Buses fill in the gaps, and GO Transit connects you to suburbs and nearby cities.

A quick glance at a map helps: Yonge Street runs north–south through the heart of downtown. East of Yonge, streets are named; west of Yonge, they're numbered. Queen Street East and West form the city's main east–west artery for shops and nightlife. The lakefront marks the southern edge—beyond that lies the Harbourfront and ferry docks.

Chapter 2: Planning Your Trip

Best Time to Visit (Weather, Festivals, Off-Season)

Toronto's four seasons each offer a different side of the city. Choosing when to visit shapes your experience—from patio brunches to skating under twinkling lights.

Spring (March–May)

As temperatures climb from near freezing in March (around 0 °C/32 °F) to mild days in May (15 °C/59 °F), Toronto shakes off winter's chill. High Park's cherry blossoms burst into pink in late April, drawing photographers and picnic-goers. Hotel rates are still low, and lines at popular spots like the Distillery District are short. Bring layers—a light sweater, waterproof jacket, and scarf cover chilly mornings and sudden rain showers. One April, I wandered Kensington Market in a T-shirt by afternoon, then zipped up my jacket as a cold front rolled in at dusk.

Summer (June–August)

Summer is festival season and peak tourism. Daily highs hover between 20 °C and 30 °C (68–86 °F), with long daylight stretching well past 9 PM. Pride Toronto in late June turns Chrch and Wellesley into a rainbow street party. Caribana (Toronto Caribbean Carnival) in early August fills the streets with steel-pan bands and colorful costumes. Summerlicious offers prix-fixe menus at top restaurants in July. Because crowds swell, book tours and restaurants at least a month ahead. If you're flexible, aim for early June or late August to dodge the worst of the crowds while still enjoying warm weather.

Fall (September–November)
By September, the air turns crisp (10–20 °C/50–68 °F) and ravine trails blaze with red and gold leaves. TIFF (Toronto International Film Festival) takes over early September— perfect if you love film, but plan weeks in advance for screenings. After mid-October, hotel rates drop and crowds thin. Fall is ideal for waterfront strolls, bike rides along Lake Ontario, or sampling seasonal pies at St. Lawrence Market. Pack a mid-weight jacket and a warm hat; wind off the lake can bite even on sunny days.

Winter (December–February)
Winters are cold (–5 °C to –15 °C/23–5 °F) with regular snow. Yet Toronto's winter charm shines through. Lace up for skating at Nathan Phillips Square, sip hot chocolate in the Distillery District's Christmas Market, or join Winterlicious for restaurant deals in January and February. Insulated boots and a heavy coat are non-negotiable. I once underestimated winter in Toronto and found my cheap sneakers useless in slush—lesson learned to invest in proper gear.

Off-Season Perks
Late fall and early spring offer the best balance of mild weather and lower prices. You'll skip the summer lines and winter storms, and still enjoy most attractions. If festivals aren't your priority, aim for late April or mid-October to get the city to yourself and save on flights and hotels.

Visa Requirements & Entry Tips for Visitors

Before you pack your bags, check what you need to enter Canada. Rules vary by nationality and mode of arrival.

eTA (Electronic Travel Authorization)
Most visa-exempt travelers flying to Canada need an eTA. It costs CAD 7, takes minutes to apply online, and stays valid for up to five years or until your passport expires. You'll need your

passport, a credit card, and an email address. Once approved, it links electronically to your passport. U.S. green-card holders also require an eTA when flying.

Visitor Visa

If your country isn't on the visa-exempt list (for example, India, China, Nigeria), you'll need a visitor visa. Apply on the Government of Canada's website. Processing can take anywhere from two weeks to two months, so start at least six weeks before departure. You'll submit scanned documents: passport, photo, proof of funds, and a travel itinerary. Pay the fee (around CAD 100) and book a biometrics appointment if required.

Land and Sea Arrivals

Even if you drive from the U.S. or cruise into Toronto, you might still need an eTA. Check the latest rules before you cross the border. Always carry your passport and any approval letters.

At the Border

Be ready to show:

- A return or onward ticket

- Proof of funds (bank statement or credit card statement)

- Details of where you'll stay (hotel reservations or address)

- A brief itinerary or list of planned activities

Keep answers clear and honest. If you mention "visiting friends," have their address and phone number handy. Trying to work or study on a visitor status will get you turned away; apply for the correct permit instead.

Tips for Smooth Entry

- Apply for your eTA or visa early.

- Use the official Government of Canada website—avoid third-party services that add fees.

- Double-check that your passport is valid for at least six months beyond your planned return date.

- Print or screenshot approval confirmations in case cellular service is spotty at the border

How to Get There (By Air, Train, Bus, Car)

Toronto is well connected by air, rail, bus, and road. Here's how to plan your arrival.

By Air

- **Toronto Pearson International (YYZ):** Canada's busiest airport, handling flights from all over the world. After landing, head to the **UP Express** train at Terminal 1. It runs every 15 minutes to Union Station in 25 minutes for CAD 12.35 one-way.

- **Billy Bishop Toronto City Airport (YTZ):** On the island just off downtown, served by Porter and some U.S. carriers. Take the free pedestrian tunnel or short ferry to reach the mainland. From there, catch a streetcar or taxi downtown.

By Train

- **VIA Rail:** Offers service from Montreal and Ottawa multiple times daily. The **Maple Leaf** train runs from New York City to Toronto once a day. Trains arrive at Union Station, steps from the Financial District and the waterfront. Booking early scores the best fares; look for off-peak discounts.

By Bus

- **Megabus** and **Greyhound** run routes from U.S. border cities (Buffalo, Detroit) and Ontario towns. They arrive at the downtown bus terminal near Union Station. Buses can be slower than trains but are often cheaper if you book ahead.

By Car

- Major highways (401, 400, QEW) lead into Toronto. Traffic can be heavy during morning (7–9 AM) and evening (4–6 PM) rush hours. If you drive, consider parking outside downtown and taking the TTC or GO Transit train in—downtown parking rates can top CAD 30 per day.

- **Border crossings:** If driving from the U.S., cross at Peace Bridge (Buffalo), Rainbow Bridge (Niagara Falls), or Windsor–Detroit Tunnel. Lines vary—check live updates online and aim for off-peak hours.

Insider Tips

- If your flight lands late, the UP Express runs until about 1 AM. After that, night buses (Route 300) cover the Pearson-downtown route but take longer.

- For budget travelers, coach bus specials can drop fares below CAD 20 if you book weeks ahead.

- Always factor in extra time for customs and baggage claim—Pearson can be busy during peak travel seasons.

Transportation Within Toronto (TTC, Biking, Walking)

Once you arrive, Toronto's mix of subways, streetcars, buses, bike lanes, and walkable neighborhoods makes getting around easy.

TTC (Toronto Transit Commission)

- **Subway:** Lines 1 (Yonge–University), 2 (Bloor–Danforth), 3 (Scarborough), and 4 (Sheppard) cover most key areas. Trains run every 2–5 minutes during rush hours, 5–10 minutes off-peak.

- **Streetcars:** Iconic red streetcars run on major streets like King, Queen, and Spadina. They share lanes with cars, so they can slow down in traffic. Look for digital signs at stops to time your ride.

- **Buses:** Fill gaps where subway or streetcar lines don't reach, especially in the outer boroughs.

Fares & Passes

- **Presto card:** Tap on and off for CAD 3.35 per ride. Load online or at stations.
- **Day pass:** CAD 13.50 for unlimited travel over 24 hours— great if you plan multiple trips.
- **Weekly pass:** CAD 43.75 for unlimited rides Monday through Sunday.

Biking

- **Bike Share Toronto:** Rent bikes at hundreds of stations. Rates start at CAD 3.25 per 30 minutes; daily passes are CAD 10.
- Many protected bike lanes downtown and along major corridors. Always lock your bike with a sturdy U-lock, even for a quick stop.

Walking

- Downtown Toronto is highly walkable. You can stroll from Union Station through the Entertainment District to the waterfront in under 30 minutes.
- Use offline map downloads to avoid data charges or spotty service in ravines and parks.

Ride-hailing & Taxis

- Uber and Lyft operate citywide, often cheaper than taxis.
- Licensed taxis (green-and-white or blue-and-white cabs) can be flagged on the street or found at taxi stands near major hotels and transit hubs.

Pro Tips

- Download the TTC's official app or RocketMan for real-time arrivals.

- Avoid rush-hour crowds (7–9 AM, 4–6 PM) if you can—subways and streetcars get packed.

- For late-night returns, night buses cover major routes after subway hours end (around 1 AM).

Budgeting for Your Trip (Low, Mid, High)

Toronto can fit a tight backpacker's budget or a luxury traveler's wallet. Here's how to plan your daily spending.

Low Budget (CAD 70–90/day)

- **Accommodation:** Dorm bed in a hostel (CAD 30–50).

- **Food:** Street food or fast-casual spots (CAD 5–10 per meal). Grab a peameal bacon sandwich at St. Lawrence Market for under CAD 6.

- **Transport:** TTC day pass (CAD 13.50).

- **Activities:** Free walking tours, city parks, and neighborhood strolls. Budget CAD 10–15 for one paid attraction.

Mid Budget (CAD 150–200/day)

- **Accommodation:** 3-star hotel or private Airbnb (CAD 120–200).

- **Food:** Mix of casual restaurants and one sit-down meal (CAD 15–30 per meal). Try a prix-fixe lunch during Summerlicious for CAD 23.

- **Transport & Activities:** CityPASS (CAD 72) covers five major attractions—averages CAD 15 per site. Add taxis or ride-shares for CAD 20–30.

High Budget (CAD 300+/day)

- **Accommodation:** Boutique or luxury hotel (CAD 250+).
- **Food:** Fine dining (CAD 50+ per meal). Book a chef's tasting menu at Alo or Canoe.
- **Transport & Activities:** Private guided tours (CAD 100+), frequent taxis or limo services, and special events or shows (theatre, concerts).

Money-Saving Tips

- **CityPASS:** Saves up to 40 % if you hit the main sights.
- **Free Museum Evenings:** ROM is free Friday nights after 4:30 PM; AGO is free Wednesday evenings.
- **Markets & Food Halls:** Assembly Chef's Hall and St. Lawrence Market offer quality meals under CAD 15.
- **Neighborhood Eats:** Skip the tourist traps near CN Tower— walk a few blocks to Chinatown or Little India for cheaper, authentic dishes.

Packing Tips for Toronto's Seasons

Packing smart means staying comfortable and prepared, no matter when you visit.

Spring

- **Layers:** Long-sleeve shirts, thin sweaters, and a light waterproof jacket.
- **Rain gear:** Compact umbrella and water-resistant shoes.
- **Extras:** A lightweight scarf for wind and early-morning chill.

Summer

- **Clothing:** T-shirts, shorts, and a light dress or linen pants.

- **Sun protection:** Hat, sunglasses, and sunscreen—Toronto's sun can be strong by the lake.
- **Hydration:** Reusable water bottle; refill at public water stations.

Fall

- **Mid-weight layers:** Sweaters, a fleece or softshell jacket, and a scarf.
- **Footwear:** Closed-toe shoes with good traction for wet leaves.
- **Extras:** A beanie or light knit hat for cooler mornings.

Winter

- **Outerwear:** Insulated, waterproof coat with a hood.
- **Base layers:** Thermal underwear or moisture-wicking long johns.
- **Accessories:** Warm gloves, a thick scarf, wool socks, and insulated boots.
- **Extras:** Hand warmers and a sturdy umbrella for mixed precipitation.

Always Include

- **Daypack:** For water, snacks, camera, and souvenirs.
- **Tech gear:** Universal adapter (Type A/B, 120 V), portable charger, and extra charging cables.
- **Health kit:** Basic first-aid items, any prescription meds, and hand sanitizer.

Packing Tricks

- Roll clothes to save space and reduce wrinkles.
- Use packing cubes to organize outfits by day or activity.

- Wear your bulkiest items (coat, boots) on travel days to free up suitcase room.

Internet, SIM Cards, and Staying Connected

Staying online in Toronto is easy, whether you need a local SIM or just free Wi-Fi.

Prepaid SIM Cards

- **Major carriers:** Bell, Rogers, Telus offer tourist plans (2–5 GB for CAD 20–40). Purchase at airport kiosks, convenience stores, or carrier shops downtown.
  - **MVNOs:** Chatr and Public Mobile often have cheaper data-only plans—look for CAD 25 for 3 GB.

eSIM Options

  - Services like Airalo or Nomad let you buy and activate data before landing. You'll have service as soon as you step off the plane. Plans start around USD 5 for 1 GB.

Free Wi-Fi

- **Cafés and Libraries:** Most cafés (Tim Hortons, Starbucks) and all Toronto Public Library branches offer open Wi-Fi. Speeds vary—avoid large downloads.
- **Public Spots:** Some TTC stations and parts of the Waterfront have free hotspots, but connections can drop.

Pocket Wi-Fi Rental

- Ideal for groups or if you need constant high-speed access. Rent online or at the airport for CAD 5–10/day. Connect up to five devices.

Staying Secure

- Always use a VPN on public networks.

- Keep your phone locked with a PIN or fingerprint.
- Backup important documents (passport scan, itinerary) in cloud storage.

Extra Tips

- Download offline maps (Google Maps or Maps.me) before you go out.
- Carry a small power bank (10,000 mAh) so you never hunt for an outlet.
- Bookmark emergency numbers: 911 for police/ambulance, 311 for city services.

Chapter 3: Top Attractions In Toronto

CN Tower & EdgeWalk

Address: 290 Bremner Blvd, Toronto, ON M5V 3L9

Price: Observation Deck: ~CAD 38; EdgeWalk experience: ~CAD 225

How to Get There:

Take the TTC to Union Station (Line 1), then walk south on Bay St. toward Front St. W. Follow signs to the CN Tower—about a 5-minute walk.

Best Time to Visit:

Aim for weekday mornings or late afternoons. Early visits (8 – 10 AM) beat the crowds and often have clearer skies. Late-day visits (4 – 6 PM) let you catch sunset colors and see the city light up.

Why You Should Visit:

The CN Tower is Toronto's signature landmark and a feat of engineering. From the ground it looks impossibly tall; from the top, you realize why. Standing on the observation deck, you feel the city spread beneath you—Lake Ontario's blue, the downtown grid, the islands just offshore. It's a moment that sticks with you, whether you're a first-timer or a repeat visitor.

Activities & Things to Do:

- **Observation Levels:** The main LookOut Level offers panoramic windows and informative displays about Toronto's neighborhoods. Step onto the Glass Floor if you dare—standing on transparent panels 1,122 feet above the ground gives a real thrill.

- **EdgeWalk:** For a bigger rush, book the EdgeWalk. Clipped to an overhead rail, you walk hands-free around the tower's circumference. It's the world's highest full-circle, hands-free walk on a building. Guides share fun facts—like how the tower sways in wind by up to 1 foot—and capture photos so you can relive the thrill.

- **360 Restaurant:** If you want to linger, reserve a table at 360, the revolving restaurant. One full rotation takes 72 minutes, giving you ever-changing views while you dine on Canadian-inspired dishes.

Personal Anecdote & Tips:

On my first visit, I waited until just before sunset. As the sun dipped, the glass panels glowed pink, and the city lights twinkled on one by one. It was worth the slight chill up top. If you're visiting in winter, bundle up—even indoors you'll feel a breeze near the windows. And buy tickets online in advance: timed-entry slots fill up fast, especially on weekends.

Additional Info:

- **Accessibility:** Elevators take you directly to the LookOut Level; EdgeWalk participants must be physically fit and free of loose items.

- **Photography:** The deck has tripod-free rules; handheld cameras only. For the best skyline shots, aim for a clear day—visibility can stretch up to 100 miles.

- **Nearby:** Pair your visit with Ripley's Aquarium (same plaza) or a stroll along the waterfront boardwalk.

Royal Ontario Museum (ROM)

Address: 100 Queens Park, Toronto, ON M5S 2C6
Price: Adult general admission ~CAD 23; youth/senior discounts available
How to Get There:
Take the TTC to Museum Station (Line 1). Follow the

underground PATH signs to enter the museum without facing bad weather.

Best Time to Visit:
Weekday mornings (10 AM – 12 PM) are ideal. The galleries feel calm, and you can study displays without jostling crowds.

Why You Should Visit:
The ROM blends art, culture, and science under one roof. From dinosaur skeletons to Chinese jade carvings, it's a journey across time and continents. Whether you're into natural history or world cultures, there's a display that sparks curiosity.

Activities & Things to Do:

- **Dinosaur Gallery:** Walk beneath a towering T. rex skeleton. The ROM's collection includes a rare Daspletosaurus skull—its jaws look ready to snap.

- **Bat Cave:** A dimly lit room simulating a real cave with hanging bat specimens. It's equal parts eerie and fascinating.

- **Indigenous Galleries:** Learn about Canada's First Peoples through totem poles, masks, and beadwork. Audio guides share stories from Indigenous voices.

- **Special Exhibits:** Rotating exhibitions range from fashion retrospectives to interactive science shows. Check the ROM website before you go to catch limited-time events.

- **Hands-On Workshops:** Book a "Maker" session to try fossil casting or artifact handling. Great for families with kids aged 6 and up.

Personal Anecdote & Tips:
I once spent a rainy afternoon lost among the ROM's vaulted galleries. I stumbled upon a Ming Dynasty exhibit and found myself tracing the intricate porcelain patterns for nearly half an hour. If you love details, pause at the small labels—they often

hide surprising facts, like how ancient Romans used powdered mouse brains in cosmetics.

Additional Info:

- **Facilities:** On-site café and gift shop. Free Wi-Fi in the lobby.

- **Accessibility:** Wheelchair accessible, with seating throughout. Braille labels and audio tours available.

- **Tickets:** Consider the ROM+AGO combo pass if you plan to visit both institutions within a week—it saves about 20%.

Art Gallery of Ontario (AGO)

Address: 317 Dundas St W, Toronto, ON M5T 1G4
Price: Adult admission ~CAD 25; students/seniors ~CAD 19
How to Get There:
Exit Dundas Station (Line 1) and walk west on Dundas St W for about 2 minutes. The AGO's glass façade is hard to miss.

Best Time to Visit:
Weekday afternoons (1 – 4 PM) are quieter. If you go on a Thursday evening (6 – 9 PM), admission is pay-what-you-can.

Why You Should Visit:
AGO houses one of the largest art collections in North America, with a strong focus on Canadian art—from Group of Seven landscapes to Indigenous works. The building itself, redesigned by Frank Gehry, is a masterpiece of light and space.

Activities & Things to Do:

- **Canadian Collection:** See Tom Thomson's misty lake scenes and Emily Carr's forest paintings. These works capture Canada's rugged beauty.

- **European Masters:** Look for pieces by Rembrandt, Picasso, and Van Gogh. The AGO's Impressionist and post-Impressionist collection rivals many European galleries.

- **Photography Gallery:** Rotating shows highlight contemporary photographers. I once saw a stunning portrait series shot in Toronto's subway stations.
- **Galleries for Kids:** The Learning Centre offers drop-in art projects and storytelling sessions on weekends.
- **Guided Tours:** Free 45-minute tours run daily—check the board near the entrance for times.

Personal Anecdote & Tips:
On a chilly winter day, I ducked into the AGO and found myself lost in the glass-walled staircase. Sunlight streamed in, making the spiral look like a modern sculpture. If you need a break, the café upstairs has large windows overlooking Grange Park—perfect for sketching or people-watching.

Additional Info:
- **Photography:** Non-flash photos are allowed in most galleries.
- **Membership:** Annual membership pays for itself in two visits and gives discounts on workshops and store items.
- **Accessibility:** Fully accessible with elevators, wheelchairs, and descriptive audio tours.

Ripley's Aquarium of Canada

Address: 288 Bremner Blvd, Toronto, ON M5V 3L9
Price: Adult tickets ~CAD 35; family packages and youth rates available
How to Get There:
Located at the base of the CN Tower. From Union Station, walk south on Bay St., then turn left onto Bremner Blvd.

Best Time to Visit:
Weekday mornings (9 – 11 AM) offer the quietest experience. Weekend afternoons can be busy, especially with school groups.

Why You Should Visit:

Ripley's Aquarium brings marine life to landlocked Toronto. The highlight is the Dangerous Lagoon tunnel, where sharks and rays glide overhead—an immersive experience that feels like walking on the ocean floor.

Activities & Things to Do:

- **Dangerous Lagoon:** Ride the moving walkway through a 97-foot tunnel. Sharks, sea turtles, and guitarfish swim above and beside you.

- **Touch Tanks:** Gently handle starfish and horseshoe crabs under staff supervision. It's a hit with kids and curious adults.

- **Planet Jellies:** Watch colorful jellyfish drift in illuminated tanks—hypnotic and calming.

- **Ray Bay:** Watch divers feed and interact with friendly rays. Divers answer questions over a loudspeaker, so you learn while you watch.

- **Educational Talks:** Scheduled daily, covering topics like coral reef conservation and marine biology careers.

Personal Anecdote & Tips:

My nephew squealed when a small shark swam just inches above his head in the tunnel. We returned three times to watch that moment again. If you're with young children, pick up a map at the entrance—it lists feeding times and talks so you can plan your route.

Additional Info:

- **Photography:** Non-flash allowed; the tunnel lighting makes for dramatic shots.

- **Café & Shop:** A small café offers snacks and hot drinks; the gift shop has marine-themed toys and books.

- **Conservation:** Ripley's partners with marine rescue groups—look for donation bins if you want to support rehabilitation efforts.

Casa Loma

Address: 1 Austin Terrace, Toronto, ON M5R 1X8
Price: Adult admission ~CAD 30; guided tours extra
How to Get There:
Take the TTC to Dupont Station (Line 1), then catch the 127 Davenport bus eastbound to Casa Loma. Alternatively, it's a 20-minute walk uphill from St. Clair West Station.

Best Time to Visit:
Spring and summer are ideal—gardens bloom and outdoor terraces open. Fall foliage adds rich color in October.

Why You Should Visit:
Casa Loma is Toronto's only castle. Built in 1914, it offers a glimpse into a bygone era of luxury. Its Gothic Revival architecture, secret passages, and manicured gardens make it feel like a storybook come to life.

Activities & Things to Do:

- **Grand Suites:** Tour the staterooms, library, and music room. Each space is decorated with period furnishings and original artwork.

- **Secret Passages:** Find hidden doors behind bookcases and ornate panels. It's a fun scavenger hunt, especially for families.

- **Gardens & Grounds:** Stroll the Italianate gardens, complete with fountains and sculpted hedges. In summer, seasonal flower displays add vibrant color.

- **Special Events:** Casa Loma hosts evening jazz nights, Halloween haunted tours, and winter light shows—check the calendar before you go.

- **Dining:** The Garden Café offers light meals on the terrace. For a splurge, book afternoon tea in the conservatory.

Personal Anecdote & Tips:

I visited during a winter light festival. Walking through illuminated tunnels in the gardens felt magical, like stepping into a fairy tale. Wear comfortable shoes—the castle has many stairs, and the grounds are extensive.

Additional Info:

- **Accessibility:** Main floors accessible, but some upper levels require navigating stairs.

- **Photography:** Non-commercial photography is allowed; tripods are not.

- **Combo Tickets:** Pair with a nearby museum (e.g., Gardiner Museum) for a discount.

Toronto Islands & Centreville

Ferry Departure Point: Jack Layton Ferry Terminal, 9 Queens Quay W, Toronto, ON
Price: Ferry: ~CAD 8 one-way; Centreville admission: ~CAD 25 for a day pass

How to Get There:

From Union Station, walk south on Bay St. to Queens Quay. The terminal is clearly marked. Ferries run every 15–20 minutes.

Best Time to Visit:

Late spring through early fall (May–September). Weekday visits are quieter; weekends see more families.

Why You Should Visit:

The Islands feel like a world apart from downtown. You trade skyscrapers for open skies, sandy beaches, and tree-lined paths. It's the perfect mix of relaxation and family fun.

Activities & Things to Do:

- **Beaches:** Centre Island Beach and Hanlan's Point Beach offer sandy shores. Swim, sunbathe, or rent a canoe.

- **Bike & Kayak Rentals:** Rent bikes or tandem kayaks at island kiosks. A 7 km loop around the main islands takes about 1–2 hours by bike.

- **Centreville Amusement Park:** Classic rides like the carousel, Ferris wheel, and bumper cars. Ideal for kids under 12.

- **Picnics & BBQs:** Designated picnic areas with tables and grills. Bring your own food or buy from island vendors.

- **Walking Trails:** Quiet paths through natural areas—keep an eye out for migrating birds and native wildlife.

Personal Anecdote & Tips:

I once spent a cloudy afternoon biking around the islands. The ferry ride was short but scenic—the skyline framed by sailboats. Pack a picnic lunch; the concession lines can get long on weekends. If you're visiting Centreville, arrive right when it opens to avoid long queues at the ticket booth.

Additional Info:

- **Accessibility:** Wheelchair-accessible ferries and paved paths on Centre Island.

- **Seasonal:** Some facilities close in late October; check schedules in advance.

- **Wildlife:** The islands are home to rabbits and waterfowl—feed them only approved foods.

St. Lawrence Market

Address: 93 Front St E, Toronto, ON M5E 1C3
Price: Free entry; food and goods priced individually (CAD 2–20+)

How to Get There:
Take the TTC to King Station (Line 1) and walk east on King St E. The market's distinctive brick façade and green roof are easy to spot.

Best Time to Visit:
Weekday mornings (8 – 10 AM) for the freshest produce and smallest crowds. Saturdays are busiest but feature the Saturday Farmers' Market upstairs.

Why You Should Visit:
St. Lawrence Market has been running since 1803. It's a hub of local food culture—chefs shop here, families pick up weekend brunch ingredients, and tourists sample Canadian specialties.

Activities & Things to Do:

- **Peameal Bacon Sandwich:** A market classic—thick-cut back bacon rolled in cornmeal on a fresh bun. Try it at Carousel Bakery; expect a small queue but a big payoff.

- **International Flavors:** Sample cheeses from Quebec, olives from Greece, or freshly made tamales. Stalls like Buster's Sea Cove offer lobster rolls, while Rosedale's sausage vendor serves artisanal bratwurst.

- **Artisan Crafts:** Upstairs you'll find handmade pottery, jewelry, and local art—perfect for souvenirs.

- **Food Tours:** Join a guided tasting tour to learn market history and sample hidden gems.

- **Cooking Classes:** Some vendors host small-group cooking demos—book ahead to learn how to make fresh pasta or pickles.

Personal Anecdote & Tips:
On my first Saturday visit, I lined up at Carousel Bakery for the bacon sandwich. While waiting, I chatted with a local chef who told me how she sources produce here for her restaurant. Sharing tips and samples turned a simple sandwich run into a mini insider's tour. Bring small bills and coins—some vendors don't take cards for orders under CAD 10.

Additional Info:

- **Hours:** Tues–Thurs 8 AM–6 PM; Fri 8 AM–7 PM; Sat 5 AM–5 PM; Sun/Mon closed.

- **Parking:** Limited underground parking; better to use TTC or bike racks nearby.

- **Events:** The market hosts seasonal events like the Pie Competition in February.

Distillery Historic District

Address: 55 Mill St, Toronto, ON M5A 3C4
Price: Free to wander; costs for food, drink, and shopping vary
How to Get There:
Take the TTC to King Station (Line 1), then catch the 504 King streetcar east to Parliament St. Walk south on Parliament to Mill St.

Best Time to Visit:
Evenings and weekends are lively, with live music and outdoor patios. For a quieter stroll, go mid-week in the afternoon.

Why You Should Visit:
This pedestrian-only district preserves Victorian industrial architecture in a modern arts and dining hub. Cobblestone lanes, restored brick buildings, and string lights create a charming backdrop for shopping, dining, and art.

Activities & Things to Do:

- **Art Galleries & Studios:** Browse contemporary art at galleries like Thompson Landry. Watch local artists at work during First Friday Art Crawl (monthly).

- **Boutiques & Shops:** Find handmade leather goods, artisan chocolates, and vintage clothing. Soma Chocolate Lab lets you watch chocolatiers craft truffles.

- **Dining & Drinks:** From casual breweries (Mill St. Brewpub) to upscale restaurants (Cluny Bistro), there's something for every palate. Don't miss the artisanal ice cream at Soma's café.

- **Street Performances:** Musicians and magicians often set up in the courtyard. In summer, you might catch a jazz trio under the string lights.

- **Guided Walking Tours:** Learn about the district's history as a 19th-century whiskey factory and its rebirth as a cultural landmark.

Personal Anecdote & Tips:
I visited on a rainy Thursday and ducked into Balzac's Coffee for a flat white. Peering out at the wet cobbles, I felt like I'd stepped into a European village. If you're here in December, the Toronto Christmas Market transforms the district with stalls, carolers, and mulled wine—plan ahead, as tickets sell out.

Additional Info:

- **Accessibility:** Most pathways are wheelchair accessible; some older buildings have step-free entrances.

- **Parking:** Paid lots nearby; better to take public transit.

- **Events:** The district hosts the annual Icefest in February, featuring large ice sculptures and winter activities.

Yonge-Dundas Square

Address: 1 Dundas St E, Toronto, ON M5B 2R8
Price: Free public space; event costs vary
How to Get There:
Dundas Station (Line 1) exits directly onto the square. It's also well served by streetcars on Yonge and Dundas.

Best Time to Visit:
Evenings (6 – 10 PM) when digital billboards light up and events kick off. Weekend afternoons host free concerts and cultural festivals.

Why You Should Visit:
Yonge-Dundas Square is Toronto's Times Square—a hub of lights, performances, and energy. It's the perfect spot to feel the city's pulse and catch free outdoor events.

Activities & Things to Do:

- **Live Events:** Check the schedule for free concerts, dance performances, and film screenings. Past events have included Bollywood dance nights and indie band showcases.

- **Street Performers:** Jugglers, breakdancers, and living statues often entertain crowds—keep some change handy if you enjoy the show.

- **People-Watching:** Surrounded by shops like the Eaton Centre and restaurants, it's a great place to sit on the steps and watch the city flow by.

- **Photography:** Neon signs and giant screens create a dynamic backdrop—ideal for night photography.

- **Nearby Attractions:** Step into the Eaton Centre for shopping, then head north to explore Ryerson University's modern campus architecture.

Personal Anecdote & Tips:
I once stumbled upon an impromptu flash mob performing in

the square. Tourists and locals alike gathered, phones out, cheering the dancers. If you want to join in or just enjoy the vibe, grab a coffee from a nearby café and stake out a spot on the steps.

Additional Info:

- **Facilities:** Public washrooms under the square; free Wi-Fi available.

- **Accessibility:** Fully accessible with ramps and elevators to street level.

- **Safety:** The square is patrolled by community safety officers, making it feel secure even late at night.

Toronto Zoo

Address: 2000 Meadowvale Rd, Toronto, ON M1B 5K7
Price: Adult admission ~CAD 29; children/senior discounts available

How to Get There:
The zoo is about 30 minutes east of downtown by car. Take TTC bus 85 (Sheppard East) to the zoo entrance. GO Transit also runs occasional shuttles from Kennedy Station.

Best Time to Visit:
Spring and fall weekdays are ideal—animals are active in cooler weather, and crowds are smaller. Arrive at opening (9:30 AM) to catch morning feedings.

Why You Should Visit:
Covering 710 acres, Toronto Zoo is one of the largest in the world. Exhibits replicate natural habitats, offering a glimpse of animals from around the globe. It's both an educational outing and a chance to connect with wildlife.

Activities & Things to Do:

- **African Savanna:** See giraffes, zebras, and rhinos roaming in spacious enclosures. Feeding demonstrations happen daily—check the schedule on arrival.

- **Tundra Trek:** Observe polar bears and reindeer in a setting designed to mimic Arctic conditions. Large viewing windows let you watch bears swim underwater.

- **Canadian Domain:** Learn about native species like wolves, moose, and beavers. Interactive displays explain conservation efforts for endangered Canadian wildlife.

- **Kids' Zoo & Splash Pad:** Let children pet goats and sheep, then cool off at the splash pad on hot days.

- **Keeper Talks & Tours:** Sign up for behind-the-scenes tours to learn about animal care, enrichment, and veterinary work.

Personal Anecdote & Tips:

I visited on a crisp October morning. Watching a polar bear pace by the glass window, I felt a chill—not from the cold, but from awe at its size and power. Bring binoculars if you have them; some animals are best viewed from a distance. And wear comfortable walking shoes—the zoo is vast, with many paths and hills.

Additional Info:

- **Dining:** Several cafés and snack kiosks are scattered throughout. Pack your own lunch if you prefer a picnic.

- **Accessibility:** Wheelchair rentals available; most pathways are paved.

- **Seasonal Events:** The zoo hosts "ZooLights" during winter evenings—lights, displays, and hot chocolate make for a festive visit.

Chapter 4: Hidden Gems of Toronto

Graffiti Alley

Address: Rush Lane, between Spadina Avenue and Portland Street

Overview & Why Visit:
Graffiti Alley is a long, narrow laneway that serves as Toronto's open-air gallery. It stretches roughly 500 meters and features constantly changing street art—from large-scale murals to small stencils and wheat-paste posters. This ever-evolving canvas captures local voices, political commentary, and pure artistic flair. For photographers, art lovers, or anyone looking for a vivid slice of Toronto's creative spirit, Graffiti Alley delivers.

Price: Free. There is no fee to enter or wander.

Activities/Things to Do:

- **Self-guided photo tour:** Bring your camera or smartphone. Mornings have soft, even light, and few people.

- **Guided walking tours:** Local companies offer 1–2 hour tours explaining the stories behind key pieces. Tours run year-round; book online in advance.

- **Pop-up workshops:** Occasionally, community groups host free stencil or mural workshops—keep an eye on neighborhood bulletin boards or social media pages.

How to Get There:

- **By TTC:** Take Line 1 to Queen Station. Exit on the west side, walk west along Queen Street West to Spadina Avenue, then head south into Rush Lane.

- **By bike:** Bike lanes run on Richmond Street. Secure your bike near Spadina, then walk a block to the alley.

Best Time to Visit:

- **Weekday mornings (9 AM–11 AM):** Soft light for photos, minimal crowds.
- **Late spring through early fall:** Comfortable walking weather. In winter, the alley is accessible but cold, and some pieces may be covered for protection.

Practical Tips & Anecdote:
On a cool April morning, I wandered through and struck up a conversation with a muralist finishing a new piece celebrating local immigrant stories. He explained that many artists in Graffiti Alley pay homage to their cultural roots—one artist from Brazil had painted a vivid depiction of Carnival dancers. If you're lucky, you might catch a work in progress.

- **Respect the art:** Do not touch wet paint or lean on murals.
- **Wide-angle lens:** Useful for capturing large-scale works in tight spaces.
- **Comfortable shoes:** The lane is paved but uneven in spots.

Additional Info:

- No restrooms in the alley; nearby cafés on Queen Street West have public washrooms.
- Street parking is limited; public transit or bike is easier.

Guild Park and Gardens

Address: 201 Guildwood Parkway, Scarborough

Overview & Why Visit:
Guild Park and Gardens is a 45-hectare site on the Scarborough Bluffs that blends natural beauty with fragments of Toronto's architectural history. After demolition of heritage buildings in the 1960s, Guild Incorporated salvaged columns, statues, and

stonework, installing them among meadows, woodlands, and lakeside paths. It feels like wandering through an open-air museum and a serene nature reserve at once.

Price: Free entry.

Activities/Things to Do:

- **Sculpture garden:** Walk the paved loop to view Gothic arches, Ionic columns, and carved stone lions rescued from landmark buildings.

- **Picnicking:** Several grassy terraces overlook Lake Ontario—bring a blanket and lunch.

- **Hiking trails:** Short trails wind through mixed woods and wildflower meadows; birdwatching is excellent in spring.

- **Photography:** Sunrise over the bluffs and ruins makes for dramatic shots.

How to Get There:

- **By GO Train:** Lakeshore East line to Guildwood Station, then a 5-minute walk north on Guildwood Parkway.

- **By car:** Parking lot on site; accessible from Kingston Road via Guildwood Parkway.

Best Time to Visit:

- **Late spring–early fall:** Wildflowers bloom from May to July; autumn foliage peaks in October. Winter visits are possible but cold; sculptures may be dusted with snow.

Practical Tips & Anecdote:
I visited on a warm June morning and found a small family of deer grazing near a broken pediment. They stood still as I crept closer, framed by crumbling stone. Moments like these remind you that nature reclaims everything—even the grandest architecture.

- **Bring water:** No cafés on site.

- **Washrooms:** Portable facilities near the parking lot; none along trails.
- **Insect repellent:** Mosquitoes can be active in summer woods.

Additional Info:

- No formal guided tours, but QR-code signs explain each fragment's origin.
- Dogs allowed on leash; pick up after your pet.

Evergreen Brick Works

Address: 550 Bayview Avenue

Overview & Why Visit:
Evergreen Brick Works is a revitalized former brick factory turned environmental community center. It sits at the junction of the Don Valley trails and serves as a hub for farmers' markets, eco-workshops, and urban nature exploration. The site blends industrial heritage with sustainability initiatives, making it a top spot for families, outdoor enthusiasts, and green-minded travelers.

Price:

- Entry to site: Free.
- Farmers' market and workshops: Prices vary; check the Evergreen website.

Activities/Things to Do:

- **Farmers' Market:** Saturdays, 8 AM–1 PM (April–November). Local farmers, bakers, and artisans sell produce, cheese, bread, and crafts.
- **Don Valley Trails:** Rent a bike on site or bring your own. Trails range from easy paved paths to rugged singletrack.

- **Workshops & Events:** From beekeeping to native plant gardening, classes run year-round; preregistration recommended.
- **Art & Installations:** Seasonal public art and outdoor sculptures.
- **Café & Bake Shop:** On-site café serves soups, sandwiches, and pastries made with local ingredients.

How to Get There:

- **By TTC:** Bus 28 Bayview from Davisville Station (Line 1) to the Brick Works stop.
- **By car/bike:** Parking available; bike racks plentiful.

Best Time to Visit:

- **Market days (Saturday):** Arrive early for best selection.
- **Fall:** Trails lined with autumn colors.
- **Winter:** Cross-country skiing and snowshoe rentals on site (December–February).

Practical Tips & Anecdote:
On a crisp October afternoon, I cycled the Don Valley trail from Rosedale, arriving just as the farmers' market was closing. I grabbed a fresh apple fritter and a latte from the café—perfect reward after a 20-km ride.

- **Wear layers:** The valley can be cooler than downtown.
- **Book workshops early:** Popular classes fill up weeks in advance.
- **Trail map:** Grab one at the visitor desk or download from Evergreen's website.

Additional Info:

- Accessible washrooms in the main building.
- Dog-friendly; leash required.

- Events calendar on Evergreen.ca lists special fairs and art shows.

Allan Gardens Conservatory

Address: 19 Horticultural Avenue (north of Carlton & Jarvis)

Overview & Why Visit:
Allan Gardens Conservatory is one of Toronto's oldest parks, featuring six greenhouses filled with tropical palms, exotic orchids, desert cacti, and seasonal flower shows. Open since 1910, it's a lush refuge in the city core. Whether you need an indoor escape on a gray winter day or a colorful burst of blooms in early spring, this glasshouse oasis delivers.

Price: Free (donations appreciated).

Activities/Things to Do:

- **Greenhouse tours:** Self-guided exploration of Palm House, Orchid House, Tropical House, and more.

- **Seasonal displays:** Annual holiday poinsettia show (December–January) and orchid festival (February–March).

- **Photography:** The historic architecture and rare plants make for striking images.

- **Children's programs:** Occasional plant potting and gardening workshops for kids.

How to Get There:

- **By TTC:** College Station (Line 1), then walk east on College Street to Horticultural Avenue.

- **By streetcar:** 506 Carlton to Jarvis, then north one block.

Best Time to Visit:

- **Winter–early spring:** When outdoor gardens are dormant, the conservatory is at its peak.

- **Weekday afternoons:** Fewer crowds; natural light filters through the glass roof.

Practical Tips & Anecdote:

I ducked in on a snowy January day and spent an hour admiring the 130-year-old date palm—its fronds towering above me like a green cathedral. The warmth and humidity were a welcome contrast to the icy street outside.

- **Bring a light jacket:** Inside can be humid but slightly cool in shaded corners.
- **Washrooms available:** Near the Palm House entrance.
- **Check display schedule:** The City of Toronto website lists upcoming shows.

Additional Info:

- Wheelchair accessible.
- No on-site café; nearby coffee shops on Carlton Street.
- Donations help fund greenhouse maintenance and programming.

Toronto Music Garden

Address: 479 Queens Quay West, near Spadina Avenue

Overview & Why Visit:

The Toronto Music Garden is a collaboration between cellist Yo-Yo Ma and landscape designer Julie Moir Messervy. Inspired by Bach's First Suite for Unaccompanied Cello, the garden is divided into six sections, each representing a musical movement. Curving paths, themed plantings, and a performance stage make it a peaceful spot for both music and nature lovers.

Price: Free (concerts may require tickets).

Activities/Things to Do:

- **Self-guided stroll:** Follow the musical map to experience each movement's planting design.
- **Summer concerts:** Free weekly chamber music performances (June–August) on Sunday mornings.
- **Guided tours:** Harbourfront Centre offers 1-hour tours explaining the garden's design.
- **Picnicking:** Bring a blanket and enjoy a lakeside snack.

How to Get There:

- **By TTC:** 509 Harbourfront streetcar to Spadina Avenue, then walk south.
- **By bike:** Waterfront Trail passes directly by the garden.

Best Time to Visit:

- **June–August mornings:** For free concerts and cooler temperatures.
- **Spring:** Tulips and daffodils herald the garden's opening.

Practical Tips & Anecdote:

I arrived at dawn one July and watched a quartet rehearsing amid dew-dappled paths. The cello's warm tones drifted over the water—an almost surreal experience.

- **Bring your own seating:** Limited benches; a low camping chair works well.
- **Check Harbourfront Centre calendar:** Concert dates and times vary each year.
- **Sunscreen & hat:** Little shade during midday.

Additional Info:

- Accessible paths throughout.
- No washrooms on site; facilities at nearby Harbourfront Centre.

Ireland Park

Address: Queens Quay West & York Street

Overview & Why Visit:
Ireland Park is a small waterfront memorial commemorating the 1847 Irish famine immigrants who arrived in Toronto. Sculptor Rowan Gillespie created a series of bronze figures—men, women, and children—walking toward the city. The park links Toronto's history as a place of refuge with its modern identity as a multicultural metropolis.

Price: Free.

Activities/Things to Do:

- **Reflective walk:** Read plaques explaining each sculpture's story and the broader historical context.
- **Photography:** The dramatic contrast of dark bronze figures against the blue lake and skyline is striking.
- **Quiet picnics:** Limited grassy areas; benches face the water.

How to Get There:

- **By TTC:** Union Station (Line 1/Line 2); walk south on York Street to Queens Quay.
- **By streetcar:** 509 to York Street stop.

Best Time to Visit:

- **Spring and fall:** Milder weather and softer light for photos.
- **Late afternoon:** Sculptures cast long, dramatic shadows.

Practical Tips & Anecdote:
Visiting at sunset, I watched an elderly couple from the local Irish community lay flowers at the base of the mother-and-child sculpture. They told me they come every year on St. Patrick's Day to honor their ancestors—an emotional reminder of Toronto's living connections to the past.

- **Read the plaques:** Each gives context; don't just snap pictures.
- **Dress warmly:** Wind off Lake Ontario can be chilly, even in summer.

Additional Info:

- No washrooms in the park; nearby facilities at Harbourfront Centre.
- Combine with a walk along the Martin Goodman Trail for more waterfront views.

Tommy Thompson Park

Address: Leslie Street & Lake Shore Boulevard East

Overview & Why Visit:
Tommy Thompson Park—known locally as the Leslie Street Spit—is a 5-km man-made peninsula extending into Lake Ontario. Originally created from landfill, it's now a crucial urban wildlife sanctuary. Over 300 bird species have been recorded here, along with foxes, rabbits, and turtles. The park offers raw nature, open skies, and unobstructed skyline views.

Price: Free.

Activities/Things to Do:

- **Birdwatching:** Bring binoculars and a field guide. Spring and fall migrations are peak times.
- **Hiking & biking:** Unpaved trails wind along the spit; bike rentals available downtown.
- **Fishing:** Designated piers allow catch-and-release fishing (Ontario fishing license required).
- **Photography:** Sunrise over the city skyline makes for dramatic compositions.

How to Get There:

- **By TTC:** Bus 127 from Union Station to Leslie & Lake Shore, then walk east along the trail entrance.
- **By car:** Limited parking near Leslie Street; early arrival recommended.

Best Time to Visit:

- **Early morning:** Quietest time and best light for bird activity.
- **Spring/Fall:** Migration seasons bring peak diversity.
- **Avoid mid-summer midday:** Little shade and strong sun.

Practical Tips & Anecdote:

I arrived at dawn in late April and spotted a group of sandhill cranes feeding in the marsh. Their soft calls echoed over the water while the city skyline glowed pink in the distance.

- **Dress in layers:** Lake breezes can be cool year-round.
- **Bring water and snacks:** No services on the spit.
- **Leave no trace:** Pack out all garbage.

Additional Info:

- No restrooms; plan accordingly.
- Dogs allowed on leash; wildlife can be sensitive to disturbance.

Aga Khan Museum

Address: 77 Wynford Drive (at Don Mills Road)

Overview & Why Visit:

The Aga Khan Museum showcases Islamic art, Iranian ceramics, miniature paintings, and manuscripts spanning 1,400 years. Its minimalist architecture—designed by Fumihiko Maki—features clean lines, reflecting pools, and light-filled galleries. The museum fosters cross-cultural understanding through exhibitions, lectures, and musical performances.

Price:

- Adults $20; Seniors/Students $15; Children (12 & under) $10.
- Free admission Wednesdays 4 PM–8 PM.

Activities/Things to Do:

- **Permanent galleries:** Explore collections of metalwork, textiles, ceramics, and illuminated manuscripts.
- **Special exhibitions:** Rotating shows on topics like Persian photography or Mughal painting.
- **Garden & reflecting pools:** Stroll the landscaped grounds for quiet contemplation.
- **Performances & lectures:** Check the schedule for concerts, film screenings, and talks.

How to Get There:

- **By TTC:** Bus 34 Eglinton East from Eglinton Station (Line 1) to Wynford Drive; short walk west.
- **By car:** Parking available on site.

Best Time to Visit:

- **Weekday mornings:** Fewer visitors and better lighting.
- **Wednesday evenings:** Free admission, though expect larger crowds.

Practical Tips & Anecdote:
During a rainy afternoon visit, I lingered over a 16th-century Persian manuscript. The intricate gold leaf and vivid pigments looked almost modern. Later, I sat by the reflecting pool, listening to a student trio rehearse—an unexpected musical interlude that connected art across centuries.

- **Allow 2–3 hours:** The collection is extensive and rich in detail.
- **Audio guide:** Included in admission; highly recommended for context.

Additional Info:

- Museum café and gift shop on site.
- Combine with a visit to the adjacent Ismaili Centre for architecture and gardens.

Sugar Beach

Address: 11 Dockside Drive, at Lower Jarvis Street

Overview & Why Visit:
Sugar Beach is an urban park designed to evoke a tropical beach, complete with pink Muskoka chairs, striped umbrellas, and a sandy stretch. Located on Toronto's waterfront, it offers a playful, colorful spot to relax, snap photos, or dip your toes in Lake Ontario.

Price: Free.

Activities/Things to Do:

- **Relax on chairs:** Lounge under umbrellas with a view of the Toronto skyline.
- **Photography:** The contrast of pink chairs against blue water is highly Instagrammable.
- **Kayaking & paddleboarding:** Rentals available nearby; launch from the adjacent marina.
- **Picnicking:** Bring snacks; no on-site food vendors.

How to Get There:

- **By TTC:** 509 Harbourfront streetcar to Lower Jarvis stop, then a two-minute walk south.

- **By bike:** Waterfront Trail runs along Queens Quay; bike racks available.

Best Time to Visit:

- **June–early September:** Umbrellas and chairs are set up; beach open.
- **Weekday afternoons:** Fewer crowds than weekends.

Practical Tips & Anecdote:
I stopped by on a sweltering July afternoon with a friend. We rented a kayak nearby and paddled along the shoreline, then returned to Sugar Beach for cold drinks and shade under the umbrellas. It felt like a mini-vacation without leaving the city.

- **No sand play:** This beach has sand underfoot but no traditional play area.
- **No lifeguards:** Swimming isn't officially encouraged; stick to wading or water sports.

Additional Info:

- Restrooms at nearby Sugar Beach Café and public facilities along Queens Quay.
- Check Toronto Waterfront website for seasonal event listings.

Little India (Gerrard Street East)

Address: Gerrard Street East, between Greenwood Avenue and Coxwell Avenue

Overview & Why Visit:
Toronto's Little India along Gerrard Street East is a vibrant stretch of South Asian shops, restaurants, and cultural spaces. It's the city's go-to spot for authentic Indian and Sri Lankan cuisine, colorful textiles, and festive events like the annual Festival of South Asia.

Price: Free to explore; meals and shopping costs vary.

Activities/Things to Do:

- **Dining:** Feast on dosas, biryanis, samosas, and filter coffee at family-run eateries.
- **Shopping:** Browse sari shops, spice merchants, and jewelry stores.
- **Sweet shops:** Sample jalebi, gulab jamun, and barfi.
- **Festivals:** In August, the Festival of South Asia features parades, live music, and food stalls.

How to Get There:

- **By TTC:** Greenwood Station (Line 2), then a 10-minute walk east along Gerrard Street East.
- **By streetcar:** 506 Carlton to Coxwell Avenue stop.

Best Time to Visit:

- **Late afternoon–evening:** Restaurants and shops are lively, and aromas fill the air.
- **Festival season (August):** Streets close to traffic, and the community comes alive with music and dance.

Practical Tips & Anecdote:

I once ducked into a small bakery for fresh jalebi at 8 PM; the owner insisted I try them hot. That syrupy, crispy sweetness remains one of my favorite Toronto food memories.

- **Cash is handy:** Some small vendors don't accept cards.
- **Haggle gently:** At street stalls, a friendly negotiation is part of the experience.
- **Spice levels:** Ask if you want milder or extra spicy versions.

Additional Info:

- Washrooms are limited; cafés may allow patron use.
- Sunday hours vary; many shops close early or stay closed.

Chapter 5: Performing Arts: Theatre, Ballet, and Opera

Toronto's live performances bring energy and emotion you can't get online. From the sweep of a ballet to the intimacy of a new play, each venue has its own feel. I still remember the hush at the Four Seasons Centre as the curtain rose on *Swan Lake*—you could hear a pin drop. Below are four places to catch a show, with details on what to see, how to get there, and tips to make the most of your visit.

Four Seasons Centre for the Performing Arts

I still recall my first night at the Four Seasons Centre and how the dancers seemed to float across the stage.

- **Address:** 145 Queen St W, Toronto, ON M5H 1S8

- **Price:** CAD 30–150 per ticket, depending on seat and performance

- **Activities:** Full-length ballets, opera productions, occasional symphony concerts

- **How to get there:** TTC Subway to Osgoode Station (Queen St exit) or 501 Queen streetcar to Bay St; two-minute walk west

- **Best time to visit:** October–December for holiday shows; March–May for spring premieres

- **Why you should visit:** World-class acoustics and sightlines make you feel part of the action

- **Additional info:** Student rush tickets (CAD 15–25) available one hour before curtain; book six weeks ahead for popular shows like *The Nutcracker*

Royal Alexandra Theatre

Walking into the Royal Alexandra feels like stepping into history—its red velvet seats and gold-trimmed balconies still take my breath away. I once saw *Phantom of the Opera* here and felt every note in my chest.

- **Address:** 260 King St W, Toronto, ON M5V 1H9

- **Price:** CAD 25–200 per ticket, depending on production and seat

- **Activities:** Touring Broadway musicals, classic dramas, special matinees

- **How to get there:** TTC Subway to St. Andrew Station (King St exit) or King streetcar to University Ave; five-minute walk

- **Best time to visit:** November–January for festive musicals; summer matinees for lower prices

- **Why you should visit:** Canada's oldest working theatre (since 1907) adds vintage charm to every show

- **Additional info:** Guided backstage tours (CAD 10) run weekday afternoons—book online a week ahead

Buddies in Bad Times Theatre

At Buddies, I saw my first queer play and felt a connection I hadn't found in larger venues.

- **Address:** 12 Alexander St, Toronto, ON M4Y 1B7

- **Price:** CAD 20–50 per ticket

- **Activities:** Queer-focused plays, spoken-word nights, Rhubarb Festival of experimental works

- **How to get there:** 505 Dundas or 506 Carlton streetcar to Parliament St, then five-minute walk west
- **Best time to visit:** Late June for Pride-themed shows and community events
- **Why you should visit:** Intimate 200-seat house where bold new voices take center stage
- **Additional info:** Arrive early to mingle in the lobby lounge; post-show meetups let you chat with artists

Tarragon Theatre

I joined a playwright workshop at Tarragon and left with a new respect for how a script comes to life.

- **Address:** 30 Bridgman Ave, Toronto, ON M6K 1X9
- **Price:** CAD 20–60 per ticket
- **Activities:** World premieres of Canadian plays, writer development workshops, post-show talkbacks
- **How to get there:** TTC Subway to Dupont Station, then ten-minute walk north on Yonge St
- **Best time to visit:** April–June and September–November for new-season launches
- **Why you should visit:** Many plays start here before touring nationally—you see them first
- **Additional info:** Sign up for email alerts to snag discounted preview tickets; workshops fill fast

Indigenous Art & Cultural Spaces

Toronto sits on land of the Anishinaabe, Haudenosaunee, and Wendat peoples. Visiting Indigenous art spaces isn't just about seeing art—it's about connecting with living cultures and histories. I still remember the drum-making workshop at the Native Canadian Centre and how each beat told a story. Here are four places where you can learn, reflect, and support Indigenous creators in the city.

Native Canadian Centre of Toronto

Joining a powwow at the Native Canadian Centre felt like stepping into a living history lesson. During the drum workshop, I learned how each drumbeat carries meaning.

- **Address:** 16 Spadina Rd, Toronto, ON M5R 2S7
- **Price:** Admission by donation (suggest CAD 5)
- **Activities:** Rotating art exhibits, beading and drum-making workshops, monthly courtyard powwows
- **How to get there:** 506 Carlton or 510 Spadina streetcar to Spadina Rd, then two-minute walk north
- **Best time to visit:** Spring and fall when outdoor gatherings bring the centre to life
- **Why you should visit:** Community-run space where Elders share traditions directly
- **Additional info:** Check their website for free "lunch & learn" talks; arrive early for popular workshops

Sweetgrass Gallery

The first time I walked into Sweetgrass, the clean white walls let the art speak for itself. I chatted with an artist who explained the meaning behind each carving.

- **Address:** 451 Mount Pleasant Rd, Toronto, ON M4S 2N5
- **Price:** Free to browse; artwork CAD 100–5,000
- **Activities:** Contemporary Indigenous art exhibits, artist talks, occasional film screenings
- **How to get there:** TTC to Eglinton Station, then 34 Eglinton East bus to Mount Pleasant Rd
- **Best time to visit:** June–September for outdoor sculpture displays

- **Why you should visit:** Discover both emerging and established Indigenous artists in a modern setting
- **Additional info:** They ship Canada-wide—ask about framing services if you plan to buy

Art Gallery of Ontario – Indigenous Galleries
Walking through the AGO's Indigenous galleries, I was struck by the range from ancient carvings to bold new paintings. Using the Indigenous-led audio tour made each piece come alive.

- **Address:** 317 Dundas St W, Toronto, ON M5T 1G4
- **Price:** CAD 25 adult; free Wednesdays 6–9 pm
- **Activities:** Permanent collection of Inuit and First Nations art, rotating contemporary shows
- **How to get there:** TTC Subway to Queen's Park or St. Patrick, or 505 Dundas streetcar to McCaul St
- **Best time to visit:** Wednesday evenings for free entry and smaller crowds
- **Why you should visit:** One of North America's largest public collections of Indigenous art under one roof
- **Additional info:** Download the AGO app for an Indigenous-led audio tour narrated by community curators

The Bentway – Indigenous Art Park
I discovered the Bentway on a sunny afternoon and was surprised to find steel sculptures under the Gardiner Expressway.

- **Address:** Fort York Blvd & Strachan Ave, Toronto, ON M5V 3W9
- **Price:** Free
- **Activities:** Outdoor installations by Indigenous artists, guided art walks, pop-up performances

- **How to get there:** 509 Harbourfront streetcar to Fort York Blvd or 10-minute walk from Union Station
- **Best time to visit:** Late spring to early fall when public events are scheduled
- **Why you should visit:** Unique open-air gallery blending city infrastructure with Indigenous creativity
- **Additional info:** Pack a picnic—the benches and grassy spots make a nice art-filled lunch break

Street Art, Murals & Public Installations

Toronto's alleys and walls act like ever-changing galleries. One morning I wandered Graffiti Alley at dawn and watched an artist finish a vibrant portrait. That sense of discovery—turning a corner to find fresh color—makes exploring street art a city adventure. Here are four spots where you can trace Toronto's creative pulse on concrete.

Graffiti Alley

Walking through Graffiti Alley at sunrise, I watched an artist add final touches to a colorful owl mural and snapped a photo for my wall.

- **Address:** Rush Lane (between Spadina Ave & Portland St)
- **Price:** Free
- **Activities:** Self-guided mural tour, photography, sketching
- **How to get there:** TTC Subway to Queen Station; walk south on University Ave, then east on Richmond St to Spadina
- **Best time to visit:** Weekday mornings for clear walls and fewer people

- **Why you should visit:** Toronto's most famous block of street art, updated weekly by local and global artists
- **Additional info:** Wear sturdy shoes—some lanes have uneven pavement; don't touch or tag the art

Kensington Market Murals

Kensington Market's winding lanes are dotted with art that reflects its creative spirit. A mural of a jaguar behind a café inspired me to sketch right on the spot.

- **Address:** Laneways around Augusta Ave & Baldwin St
- **Price:** Free
- **Activities:** Mural hunt, guided walking tours, stops at local cafés
- **How to get there:** TTC Subway to Spadina Station, then 510 Spadina streetcar to Dundas West
- **Best time to visit:** Saturday mornings when market stalls and live music animate the streets
- **Why you should visit:** The art here celebrates diversity and community in bold colors
- **Additional info:** Grab a taco at Seven Lives (69 Kensington Ave) and sketch from their patio

Queen Street West Murals

Queen West is a hotspot for new murals and live-painting events. I once saw an artist spray-paint a huge flower across a brick wall in under an hour.

- **Address:** Queen St W between Bathurst St & Spadina Ave
- **Price:** Free
- **Activities:** Live painting, photography, shopping in indie stores
- **How to get there:** TTC 501 Queen streetcar stops along the strip

- **Best time to visit:** Late spring during Mural Festival when new pieces debut
- **Why you should visit:** Trendsetting area—artists often launch work here first
- **Additional info:** Many cafés sell prints of local murals; ask shop owners about each artist's story

York Beltline Trail Murals

The Beltline Trail mixes art and nature in a leafy corridor. I biked through and stopped to admire abstract panels hidden among trees.

- **Address:** Entry at Eglinton Ave W & Mount Pleasant Rd
- **Price:** Free
- **Activities:** Walking, cycling, mural spotting, birdwatching
- **How to get there:** TTC Subway to Eglinton Station, then 10-minute walk north on Mount Pleasant Rd
- **Best time to visit:** Early fall when leaves add extra color around the art
- **Why you should visit:** A quieter spot where art meets green space—perfect for a relaxed outing
- **Additional info:** Trail maps at each entrance; bring water and a snack for a longer walk

TIFF Bell Lightbox and the Film Scene

Toronto's film scene goes beyond blockbusters. The city hosts world-class festivals and screens rare films year-round. I still smile remembering a midnight horror screening at TIFF Bell Lightbox, then chatting with the director afterward. Here are four venues where film feels like a shared celebration, with tips on tickets, schedules, and what makes each spot special.

TIFF Bell Lightbox
Seeing an indie premiere at the Lightbox felt like joining a secret club of film lovers.

- **Address:** 350 King St W, Toronto, ON M5V 3X5
- **Price:** CAD 15–25 per ticket; ground-floor gallery free
- **Activities:** Film premieres, classic retrospectives, exhibitions, Q&A sessions
- **How to get there:** TTC Subway to Osgoode Station or 509 Harbourfront streetcar to King St
- **Best time to visit:** Early September during TIFF; any Wednesday 6–9 pm for free entry
- **Why you should visit:** You see films before general release and meet filmmakers at talks
- **Additional info:** Buy a Lightbox Pass online to save on multiple tickets; book big titles two weeks ahead

Hot Docs Ted Rogers Cinema
Watching a new documentary here opened my eyes to stories I hadn't heard before.

- **Address:** 506 Bloor St W, Toronto, ON M5S 1Y3
- **Price:** CAD 12–18 per ticket
- **Activities:** Documentary screenings year-round, director Q&As, Hot Docs Festival in April/May
- **How to get there:** TTC Subway to Spadina Station, then 506 Carlton streetcar to Bloor St
- **Best time to visit:** Late April–early May for the Hot Docs Festival
- **Why you should visit:** Canada's top venue for documentaries, with rare global films
- **Additional info:** Ask about student rush tickets day-of; arrive 30 minutes early for best seats

Revue Cinema

The Revue feels like a time capsule; its vintage seats and neon sign stand out on Roncesvalles.

- **Address:** 400 Roncesvalles Ave, Toronto, ON M6R 2M9
- **Price:** CAD 10–15 per ticket
- **Activities:** Classic-film nights, repertory series, community screenings
- **How to get there:** 505 Dundas streetcar to Roncesvalles Ave or 504 King streetcar
- **Best time to visit:** Wednesday midnight shows and Sunday matinees for fewer crowds
- **Why you should visit:** Historic neighbourhood cinema with retro charm and low prices
- **Additional info:** Cash only at the snack bar; bring change for popcorn and drinks

Royal Cinema

I first discovered Royal Cinema when a friend dragged me to an indie animation showcase—it felt fresh and different.

- **Address:** 608 College St, Toronto, ON M6G 1B6
- **Price:** CAD 10–13 per ticket
- **Activities:** Indie premieres, cult-film series, animation showcases
- **How to get there:** Subway to Bathurst Station, then 505 Dundas streetcar to College St
- **Best time to visit:** Weekday evenings during monthly themed series
- **Why you should visit:** Intimate 400-seat house that champions small and experimental films
- **Additional info:** Free street parking after 6 pm; bring a sweater for cool screening rooms

Live Music Venues and Indie Bands

Toronto's live-music circuit is where you can catch tomorrow's stars before they blow up. I spent an evening at the Horseshoe Tavern years ago, and I still brag about discovering a band there that later sold out stadiums. Whether you love folk, punk, or electronic beats, these four spots offer an up-close experience you won't get from headphones.

The Horseshoe Tavern

My first show at the Horseshoe was a raw punk set that shook the building—every beat felt alive.

- **Address:** 370 Queen St W, Toronto, ON M5V 2A2

- **Price:** CAD 10–25 cover, depending on show

- **Activities:** Rock, punk, folk gigs; open-mic nights; occasional comedy

- **How to get there:** TTC 501 Queen streetcar to Spadina Ave, then walk south one block

- **Best time to visit:** Weeknights when emerging artists headline for smaller crowds

- **Why you should visit:** Legendary venue since 1947—intimate stage and history in every brick

- **Additional info:** Arrive early to claim a front-rail spot; sound is loud—bring earplugs

Lee's Palace

Lee's Palace feels like two venues in one—indie rock downstairs and dance nights upstairs. I saw an alt band there that later played sold-out shows.

- **Address:** 529 Bloor St W, Toronto, ON M5S 1Y4

- **Price:** CAD 12–30 cover, based on act

- **Activities:** Indie-rock and alternative shows; upstairs DJ and dance events

- **How to get there:** Subway to Bathurst Station, then seven-minute walk west on Bloor St
- **Best time to visit:** Friday and Saturday nights for headliner acts
- **Why you should visit:** Two floors mean you can switch from live band to dance party
- **Additional info:** Late-night fries and poutine at the kitchen window; cash only

The Danforth Music Hall

The Danforth Music Hall's high ceilings and dance floor make big acts feel close. I once danced to an electronic set that kept me moving for hours.

- **Address:** 147 Danforth Ave, Toronto, ON M4K 1N2
- **Price:** CAD 20–60 per ticket
- **Activities:** Touring acts across genres—jazz, electronic, hip-hop
- **How to get there:** Subway to Broadview Station, then 504 King streetcar east to Danforth Ave
- **Best time to visit:** Fall and spring tours when major names swing through town
- **Why you should visit:** Historic theatre with a roomy dance floor and good sightlines
- **Additional info:** Sign up for the venue's mailing list for early ticket access and discounts

The Drake Hotel

The Drake Hotel blends art, food, and music across multiple levels. I saw a folk duo in the basement, then headed up to the rooftop DJ set.

- **Address:** 1150 Queen St W, Toronto, ON M6J 1J3
- **Price:** Free–CAD 20 cover on some nights

- **Activities:** Live sets in the basement, rooftop parties, art shows in the lobby
- **How to get there:** TTC 501 Queen streetcar to Dufferin St, then walk south two blocks
- **Best time to visit:** Summer months (May–September) for rooftop concerts
- **Why you should visit:** A cultural hub where music, art, and food come together
- **Additional info:** Basement shows don't take advance tickets—line up by 8 pm to guarantee entry

Creative Festivals: Nuit Blanche, Fringe, Contact Photography Festival,Luminato Festival

Toronto's festival scene brings art to streets, stages, and screens. I still remember wandering through installations at 3 AM during Nuit Blanche—it felt like magic in the dark. Summer brings the Fringe and photo exhibits, and Luminato lights up theatres citywide. Here are four festivals that showcase Toronto's creative pulse, with details on tickets, schedules, and tips for getting the most out of each.

Nuit Blanche
My first Nuit Blanche felt like a citywide scavenger hunt—giant light sculptures and pop-up performances everywhere I looked.

- **When & Where:** First Saturday of October; focus on Queen West, Waterfront, and downtown laneways
- **Price:** Free
- **Activities:** All-night art installations, dance and music performances, artist talks, food trucks

- **How to get there:** TTC offers free overnight service on 501, 504, and 510 streetcars; some subway stations stay open

- **Best time to visit:** Midnight–4 AM for fewer crowds and clear views of installations

- **Why you should visit:** The city transforms into an open-air gallery—every corner holds a surprise

- **Additional info:** Download the Nuit Blanche app for maps and event details; pick up printed guides at Union Station

Toronto Fringe Festival

At my first Fringe show, I saw a 15-minute comedy that made me laugh until I cried—this festival is full of surprises.

- **When & Where:** Mid-July, venues across downtown, including Theatre Passe Muraille and Bad Dog Theatre

- **Price:** CAD 12–15 per show; festival pass CAD 90 for ten shows

- **Activities:** Short plays, improv, cabaret, musical performances, late-night shows

- **How to get there:** Subway to Spadina or Bathurst, then walk to Queen and Adelaide venues

- **Best time to visit:** Opening weekend for brand-new shows before they sell out

- **Why you should visit:** Affordable access to fresh, edgy theatre and direct talks with creators

- **Additional info:** Volunteer as a Fringe Ambassador to earn free tickets in exchange for ushering

Contact Photography Festival

Walking through Contact's outdoor exhibits, I was struck by a giant projection of city scenes on a blank wall.

- **When & Where:** May, in galleries, public spaces, and pop-up venues across Toronto
- **Price:** Mostly free; some gallery openings CAD 5–10
- **Activities:** Outdoor photo installations, gallery exhibitions, artist talks, walking tours
- **How to get there:** TTC streetcars 501, 504, and 505 cover most downtown venues; some exhibits on Queen's Quay require a short walk
- **Best time to visit:** Weekday afternoons for better light and fewer crowds
- **Why you should visit:** World's largest photography festival—see everything from street snaps to large-scale projections
- **Additional info:** Many exhibits stay up through June—plan a weekend crawl to hit multiple sites

Luminato Festival

I first saw a dance piece at Luminato in the Distillery District—performers moved inside shipping containers, and the effect was unforgettable.

- **When & Where:** Mid-June, venues citywide, including Harbourfront Centre, Distillery District, and major theatres
- **Price:** CAD 20–60 per ticket; some outdoor shows free
- **Activities:** Theatre, dance, music, visual art, large-scale installations, workshops
- **How to get there:** TTC subway and streetcars to Union, King, Queen, and Exhibition Place
- **Best time to visit:** Opening weekend for headline events and free outdoor concerts at Harbourfront
- **Why you should visit:** International and local artists collaborate on works you can't see anywhere else

- **Additional info:** Family Day usually offers free kids' workshops—check the schedule for community events

Local Authors, Bookstores & Literary Toronto

Toronto's literary scene is full of cozy nooks and passionate readers. I discovered TYPE Books on a rainy afternoon, joined a poetry reading, and left with new friends and a stack of books. Whether you love fiction, poetry, or essays, these four spots connect you with writers and stories that go beyond the mainstream.

TYPE Books

TYPE Books feels like a living room for readers—comfy chairs, a back room for readings, and shelves stacked with Canadian work. I met a local poet there and still follow her writing.

- **Address:** 883 Queen St W, Toronto, ON M6J 1G3

- **Price:** Books CAD 15–40; most events free

- **Activities:** Curated Canadian fiction and poetry, author readings, book launches, open-mic nights

- **How to get there:** TTC 501 Queen streetcar to Gladstone Ave, walk south one block

- **Best time to visit:** Thursday evenings for readings; weekend afternoons for browsing

- **Why you should visit:** You'll find titles you won't see in chains and meet emerging writers

- **Additional info:** Sign up for their newsletter for event schedules; arrive early for limited seating

Book City

Book City on the Danforth has a café in the back and free

Wi-Fi—perfect for diving into a new book. I wrote my first travel-guide chapter there over a latte.

- **Address:** 348 Danforth Ave, Toronto, ON M4K 1N1
- **Price:** Books CAD 10–35; workshops CAD 20–50
- **Activities:** Author talks, writing workshops, staff picks displays, café seating
- **How to get there:** Subway to Broadview Station, then 504 King streetcar east to Danforth Ave
- **Best time to visit:** Sunday afternoons when the café is open and the shop is quiet
- **Why you should visit:** A community hub with comfy chairs, power outlets, and friendly staff
- **Additional info:** Bring your laptop to write in the café; check bulletin boards for writing groups

Another Story Bookshop
Another Story focuses on social justice and BIPOC voices. I bought a wrapped "blind date" book there and it turned out to be my new favorite novel.

- **Address:** 978 Queen St W, Toronto, ON M6J 1H1
- **Price:** Books CAD 12–45; monthly author events free
- **Activities:** Themed book clubs, poetry slams, children's story hours, book swaps
- **How to get there:** TTC 501 Queen streetcar to Dufferin St, then walk south two blocks
- **Best time to visit:** Wednesday evenings for Spine Poetry open-mic nights
- **Why you should visit:** Find underrepresented voices and support an indie community store
- **Additional info:** Ask staff about their "blind date with a book" surprises—fun for gifts

Harbourfront Centre Writers' Series

Hearing an author read by the lake adds extra magic. I once stayed after a talk to ask about their writing process.

- **Address:** 235 Queens Quay W, Toronto, ON M5J 2G8

- **Price:** CAD 10–20 per event; some talks free

- **Activities:** Readings by international and Canadian authors, panel discussions, book launches

- **How to get there:** TTC 509 Harbourfront streetcar to Queens Quay

- **Best time to visit:** March–May for peak reading season and larger lineups

- **Why you should visit:** Intimate setting with views of Lake Ontario—ideal for book lovers

- **Additional info:** Combine with a boardwalk stroll or a snack at the lakeside café afterward

Chapter 6: Food & Drink Scene

Iconic Toronto Eats

Toronto's food scene has a few dishes you simply can't skip. These comfort foods pop up at busy markets, small shops, and late-night carts. Trying them is like tasting Toronto's history and everyday life. On my first visit, I found myself planning entire days around these bites—starting with a peameal bacon sandwich at dawn and ending with poutine after midnight. You'll see locals queue in the rain and swap tips on the best spots. Below, we'll dig into three must-try items: the peameal bacon sandwich, poutine, and the street hot dog.

Peameal Bacon Sandwich

- **Where:** Carousel Bakery, St. Lawrence Market (93 Front St. E)

- **Price:** CAD 8–10 (cheese +1, mustard free)

- **Best Time:** Weekday mornings, just before the 8 AM opening

- **Why Try It:** This sandwich dates back to the 1800s when William Davies cured back bacon in cornmeal. The cornmeal crust locks in juices, giving a perfect balance of salt and smoke.

- **Real-Life Tip:** I arrived at 7:50 AM one rainy Tuesday. By 8:15 AM, the line wrapped around the stall. Grab a spot at a communal table and chat with regulars—they'll share other market gems.

- **Additional Info:** Carousel sells peameal by the pound (around CAD 12/lb) if you want to cook at home. Both cash and card are accepted.

Poutine

- **Where:** Poutini's House of Poutine, Queen West (1112 Queen St. W)
- **Price:** CAD 9 for classic; CAD 13–15 for loaded versions
- **Best Time:** After 10 PM on weekends (post-bar crowds)
- **Why Try It:** Fries topped with squeaky cheese curds and rich gravy are pure comfort. Poutini's sources curds fresh from Quebec twice weekly, so they still squeak.
- **Real-Life Tip:** I grabbed the "Mexican" poutine after a concert. The spicy chorizo and jalapeños cut through the gravy's richness perfectly.
- **Additional Info:** Vegetarian gravy and gluten-free fries (+CAD 1) are available. If the line's too long, Smoke's Poutinerie at Yonge-Dundas (1 Dundas St. W) is a solid backup.

Street Hot Dog

- **Where:** Carts near King & Bay, King & University, and other office hubs
- **Price:** CAD 2.50–3.50 (add "all-dressed" +CAD 0.50)
- **Best Time:** 12:30 PM–1:30 PM (lunch rush)
- **Why Try It:** These carts are part of Toronto's daily rhythm. The simple dog with ketchup and mustard hits the spot when you need a quick, cheap meal.
- **Real-Life Tip:** I skipped the subway at King Station and found "Seranno's Street Dog" cart. The vendor suggested extra mustard—small tweak, big flavor.

- **Additional Info:** Carts often close by 2 PM and take cash only. Look for halal or Polish sausage options if you want a twist, or check the Street Eats app for vegan dogs.

Practical Advice

Carry cash and small bills—many carts prefer them. Use a Presto card or tokens to reach St. Lawrence Market (King Station) and Queen West (Queen Station). To avoid weekend lines at Carousel and Poutini's, aim for weekday mornings or late nights. If you're short on time, consider a guided food tour for insider tips. Finally, strike up a conversation in line—locals often share news of pop-up carts and secret specials. With these bites, you'll taste Toronto's heart, one plate at a time.

Multicultural Cuisines

Toronto's neighborhoods are like mini food festivals, each showcasing a different corner of the globe. You can spend one afternoon in Little Italy, savoring fresh pasta, then hop on the subway for dim sum in Chinatown. I planned my meals by neighborhood on my first visit, and it turned every meal into an adventure. Below are three areas you won't want to miss: Little Italy, Chinatown, and Greektown.

Little Italy (College Street)

- **Where:** College Street between Bathurst & Ossington
- **Spot:** Enoteca Sociale (1280 Dundas St. W)
- **Price:** CAD 18–25 per entrée; gelato CAD 4 per scoop
- **Best Time:** Thursday–Saturday evenings (reserve ahead)
- **Why Try It:** Enoteca serves fresh pasta made daily. On a cool March night, I shared cacio e pepe and tagliatelle Bolognese with friends. The owner even brought us a taste of his grandmother's tiramisu recipe.

- **Additional Info:** For a quick slice, Café Diplomatico (59 College St.) offers pizza for CAD 3.50 and espresso for CAD 2.50. Look for gelato carts on the sidewalk in summer.

Chinatown (Spadina & Dundas)

- **Where:** Spadina Ave from College to Dundas
- **Spot:** Rol San (323 Spadina Ave)
- **Price:** CAD 5–7 per dim sum basket
- **Best Time:** Weekday lunch, before 11 AM
- **Why Try It:** Shared tables and push-cart service create a lively scene. I arrived at 10 AM on a rainy Tuesday and snagged a front-row seat to the dumpling parade.
- **Additional Info:** Try Mother's Dumplings (421 Spadina Ave) for jiaozi (CAD 7 for six) and BBQ King (455 Spadina Ave) for roast duck (CAD 10+). Stock up on dried mushrooms and lotus root at nearby grocery stalls.

Greektown (The Danforth)

- **Where:** Danforth Ave from Broadview to Jones
- **Spot:** Mezes (1692 Danforth Ave)
- **Price:** CAD 10–18 per dish; loukoumades CAD 5
- **Best Time:** Summer evenings (patio season)
- **Why Try It:** On a July Friday, locals danced in the courtyard as we dug into saganaki and chicken souvlaki. The fresh tzatziki made every bite.
- **Additional Info:** Don't miss the Taste of the Danforth festival each August—street food, music, and dancing draw over a million visitors.

Practical Advice

Take the TTC: College Station for Little Italy, Spadina for Chinatown, and Broadview for Greektown. Wear comfortable shoes—you'll wander between shops and side streets. If a restaurant doesn't take reservations, arrive early or expect to wait. For a deeper dive, book a guided food tour—most run CAD 50–70 and include tastings at multiple spots. Finally, carry cash for small cafes and carts. With these neighborhoods, you'll taste Toronto's global spirit in every bite.

Must-Try Street Food and Food Trucks

Queen West Poutine Truck

Poutine is Canada's unofficial comfort food: crispy fries, squeaky cheese curds, and rich gravy all piled together. At Queen West Poutine Truck, you get that classic combo with a twist of Toronto energy. The black-and-yellow truck parks just east of Spadina, near Graffiti Alley, so you can grab a hot plate and wander through the city's famous street art.

Where & Price: A small order runs $8, a medium $10, and a large $12. You'll see the menu painted on the side of the truck. They accept tap and card, but smaller bills come in handy if the machine glitches.

What to Expect: They hand-cut fresh russet potatoes on site, frying them until golden and tender. The cheese curds arrive straight from a local dairy, so they still squeak when you bite. Their gravy is a house recipe—meaty and savory, but not too salty. You can customize with pulled pork (+$3) or mushroom gravy for vegetarians (+$2).

Best Time to Visit: After 9 PM on weeknights, when the bar crowd spills onto Queen West. The line moves quickly, usually under 10 minutes. If you go before 8 PM, you'll have fewer people, but the truck only opens around dinner.

Why You Should Try It: Poutine is the ultimate late-night treat in Toronto. One bite of those hot fries drenched in gravy makes you forget the cold air. I remember grabbing a small order after a live show at the Drake—what started as a snack turned into dinner, and I ended up sharing with a friend who declared it the best poutine they'd ever had.

Practical Tips:

- **Seating**: There's no seating at the truck. Bring it to nearby benches or grab a spot in Graffiti Alley for a colorful backdrop.
- **Sharing**: The small size can feed two if you're pairing with other snacks A medium is enough for one big appetite.
- **Timing**: If you catch the truck on a Friday night, lines can stretch around the corner. Grab a coffee from the café next door and enjoy a quick stroll until your turn.
- **Extras**: Hot sauce and malt vinegar packets are available on request. They're perfect if you like an extra kick.

Queen West Poutine Truck captures the city's love for hearty street food. It's simple, filling, and always hits the spot—no matter the hour.

Seoul Street Kitchen (Korean BBQ Taco)

When Korean and Mexican flavors collide, you get Seoul Street Kitchen's famous BBQ taco. Picture tender strips of marinated bulgogi or spicy pork tucked into a warm tortilla, then topped with crunchy kimchi slaw. It's a perfect example of Toronto's multicultural mash-ups.

Where & Price: You'll find the neon-lit truck on King Street East near Parliament. Tacos are $5 each, or grab three for $14. They accept card and tap.

Menu Highlights: The Bulgogi Special features sweet-and-savory beef, while the Spicy Pork option brings a chili kick. Vegans can choose tofu marinated in gochujang. All tacos come with a scoop of kimchi slaw and a drizzle of creamy sriracha mayo.

Best Time to Visit: Weekday lunch (11:30 AM–2 PM) before the office rush. You'll still see a line, but it moves fast—five minutes or less. On weekends, the truck often closes early after selling out.

Why You Should Try It: These tacos pack big flavor in a small package. I first tried them on a brisk afternoon and was surprised by how the warm tortilla held up under the juicy filling. The kimchi slaw adds a fresh crunch that keeps each bite interesting.

Practical Tips:

- **Extra Slaw**: Ask for a double portion of slaw if you like texture contrast. It won't cost extra.

- **Seating**: Limited to a few picnic tables. If they're full, head to the grassy patch across the street.

- **Dietary Needs**: Gluten-free tortillas are available on request. The tofu taco is a solid vegan choice.

- **Combo Deals**: On Wednesdays, they run a special: three tacos plus a drink for $18.

Seoul Street Kitchen shows how Toronto street food can be bold, creative, and deeply satisfying. Don't miss it if you love flavor-packed bites.

Island Flavors Jerk Chicken

Nothing warms you up on a chilly Toronto morning like a plate of Island Flavors' jerk chicken. This stall inside St. Lawrence Market serves authentic Caribbean flavors: smoky, spicy chicken piled over rice and peas.

Where & Price: Find Island Flavors in the south entrance of St. Lawrence Market on Front Street East. A full plate is $12, half-plate $8. Cash and cards accepted.

What to Expect: They marinate the chicken overnight in a blend of Scotch bonnet peppers, allspice, thyme, and garlic. You'll taste the heat first, then the sweet and savory notes. The rice and peas—coconut-infused rice with kidney beans—balance the spice.

Best Time to Visit: Saturday mornings around 10 AM, when the market is lively. Lines form quickly, especially when a cold snap hits.

Why You Should Try It: Caribbean food is all about bold seasoning, and this jerk chicken hits every note. I tried it on a rainy Saturday and stood under the market canopy, savoring each spicy bite. By the time I finished, I felt warm from the inside out.

Practical Tips:

- **Line Entertainment**: While waiting, browse nearby stalls selling fresh produce and baked goods.

- **Heat Level** If you can't handle too much spice, ask for "medium" instead of "hot." They'll adjust the pepper ratio.

- **Sides**: Try the fried plantains (+$2)—they're sweet, soft, and perfect with jerk.

- **Market Hours**: The market closes at 5 PM on Saturdays and is closed Sundays.

Island Flavors Jerk Chicken brings a taste of the Caribbean right into Toronto's heart. It's hearty, spicy, and the perfect antidote to a chilly morning.

Sahara Shawarma

For a taste of the Middle East, Sahara Shawarma's truck on University Avenue at Dundas is hard to beat. They roast lamb and chicken on a vertical spit, shaving thin slices into warm pita with garlic sauce and pickles.

Where & Price: The blue-and-white truck parks midday. Wraps cost $7 for chicken and $9 for lamb. Plates (no bread) are $10. They take card, tap, and cash.

Menu Details: Each wrap includes marinated meat, house-made garlic sauce, pickled turnips, and cucumber slices. You can add extra hot sauce or tahini for free.

Best Time to Visit: Late afternoon (3 PM–5 PM), after the lunch rush and before the dinner crowd.

Why You Should Try It: Shawarma is all about simple ingredients cooked right. The lamb is tender and slightly charred, and the garlic sauce is creamy without overpowering. I once grabbed a chicken wrap on a sunny afternoon and ate it on a bench nearby—one of the best quick lunches I've had in the city.

Practical Tips:

- **Gluten-Free**: Ask for a plate instead of a wrap. The meat and salad stand alone.

- **Extra Veggies**: They'll toss in lettuce and tomato if you request.

- **Seating**: Limited; try the benches at Simcoe Park across the street.

- **Speed**: The line moves quickly. Even if there are ten people ahead, you'll get your wrap in under seven minutes.

Sahara Shawarma shows that fast food can be fresh, healthy, and full of flavor. It's a go-to when you need a quick, satisfying meal.

The Big Cheese Truck (Grilled Cheese)

Who doesn't love grilled cheese? The Big Cheese Truck elevates this childhood favorite with gourmet ingredients and inventive combos. Think smoked cheddar with caramelized onions or brie with apple slices.

Where & Price: The bright yellow truck parks near Roy Thomson Hall at King and John. Sandwiches range from $8 to $12. They accept cards and tap.

Menu Highlights: The Triple Cheese Melt combines cheddar, mozzarella, and Swiss. The Brie & Apple pairs creamy brie with thinly sliced apples and honey. Add tomato soup shooter (+$3) for dipping.

Best Time to Visit: Early evening (5 PM–7 PM), just before concert crowds arrive. They also appear around matinee breaks at the theatre.

Why You Should Try It: Grilled cheese is comfort food, and this truck knows how to make it memorable. I tried the Brie & Apple after a winter walk along the waterfront—the sweet and savory combo felt like a warm hug.

Practical Tips:

- **Soup Pairing**: The tomato soup shooter is small but rich—perfect for sharing.
- **Add-Ons**: Bacon or jalapeños (+$2) take your sandwich up a notch.
- **Seating**: A few folding stools sit beside the truck. If they're full, step into the nearby parkette.
- **Dietary Notes**: Gluten-free bread is available on request.

The Big Cheese Truck proves that simple ingredients, treated well, can become something special. It's perfect for a cozy meal on the go.

El Trompo (Authentic Tacos)

If you're craving traditional Mexican tacos, El Trompo delivers. Their red-and-green striped canopy on Queen West at Ossington signals authentic al pastor, carnitas, and lengua tacos.

Where & Price: Tacos cost $3 each or four for $10. They take cash and tap payments.

What to Expect: Meat is sliced off a vertical spit and tucked into two soft corn tortillas. Each taco comes with cilantro, onion, and a choice of red or green salsa. Lime wedges and radish slices are on the side.

Best Time to Visit: Thursdays through Saturdays, 6 PM–9 PM. They often sell out by 10 PM.

Why You Should Try It: These tacos taste like they came straight from Mexico City's street stands. I remember showing up around 7 PM on a Friday and chatting with locals in line. By the time I ate my tacos, I felt like part of the neighborhood.

Practical Tips:

- **Arrive Early**: For lengua (beef tongue), show up by 7 PM— otherwise it's gone.

- **Salsa Heat**: The red salsa is spicier; try a small taste first.

- **Seating**: No chairs—grab a curb or picnic table nearby.

- **Sides**: They sometimes sell esquites (corn cups) for $5.

El Trompo proves that simple tacos, done right, are unbeatable. Bring friends and sample different fillings for a full experience.

Green Falafel Truck (Vegan Falafel)

Toronto's Kensington Market is home to Green Falafel Truck, where crispy chickpea falafels meet creamy hummus and fresh veggies—all wrapped in pita.

Where & Price: Find the bright green truck on Augusta Avenue. Wraps are $9 each. They accept cards, tap, and cash.

Menu Options: The classic wrap includes six falafel balls, hummus, tahini, pickled turnips, and salad. You can add hot sauce or za'atar seasoning at no extra cost.

Best Time to Visit: Sunday brunch (10 AM–1 PM), when the market buzz is at its peak.

Why You Should Try It: Falafel is a filling vegan option, and this truck does it well. I grabbed a wrap on a sunny Sunday and sat under a tree in the market. The crunch of the falafel and tang of the pickles made every bite lively.

Practical Tips:

- **Gluten-Free**: Request a lettuce wrap instead of pita.

- **Extra Sauce**: Don't be shy—ask for extra tahini or hot sauce.

- **Seating**: Lots of benches around the market. Grab a spot early on busy days.

- **Drinks**: They sell homemade mint lemonade for $3—perfect with the wrap.

Green Falafel Truck shows that vegan street food can be tasty, hearty, and satisfying. It's a market staple you won't want to miss.

Steam Wagon (Bao Buns & Dumplings)

On a warm evening by the lake, Steam Wagon's pastel-blue trailer on Queens Quay is a welcome sight. Their fluffy bao buns and handmade dumplings bring Asian street food to Toronto's waterfront.

Where & Price: The trailer sits near Harbourfront Centre. Bao buns are $6 each; six dumplings cost $5. They accept card, tap, and cash.

Menu Details: Pork belly bao comes with hoisin, cucumber, and scallions. Veggie dumplings feature mushrooms and cabbage. You can add chili oil or soy sauce at the counter.

Best Time to Visit: Early evening (5 PM–7 PM) during summer festivals, when the waterfront is busy.

Why You Should Try It: The contrast of soft bao and rich pork belly is irresistible. I tried one on a breezy night, then wandered along the water. The light sea air balanced the bun's richness.

Practical Tips:

- **Check Dates**: They pop up seasonally. Follow their Instagram for schedules.

- **Seating**: Picnic tables line the waterfront; snag one quickly.

- **Pairing**: Grab a craft beer from a nearby vendor to cut through the richness.
- **Takeaway**: If it's crowded, order ahead via their app for quick pickup.

Steam Wagon proves that you don't need a brick-and-mortar to serve memorable Asian bites. Their bao and dumplings are perfect for a lakeside snack.

Vegetarian & Vegan Spots

Toronto's plant-based scene has grown fast. From build-your-own bowls to upscale vegan fusion, the city offers dishes that satisfy without feeling like a trade-off. During the annual Vegandale Festival each July, food trucks line Exhibition Place, serving jackfruit tacos and vegan ice cream. On my first week exploring, I was impressed by how creative and filling these meals could be. Below are two standout spots and tips for discovering more.

Fresh on Spadina

- **Where:** 147 Spadina Ave
- **Price:** CAD 12–16 for bowls; smoothies CAD 7+
- **Best Time:** Weekday lunch (11 AM–2 PM)
- **Why Try It:** Build-your-own bowls let you mix quinoa, black beans, avocado, and chipotle dressing into a balanced meal. Their "Power Bowl" kept me energized for afternoon exploring.
- **Additional Info:** Loyalty card gets you a free bowl after five. Check social media for seasonal specials. Limited seating means takeout is a good backup.

Planta Queen

- **Where:** 1 Bloor St. W, Yorkville

- **Price:** CAD 20–30 per entrée; brunch CAD 18–22; cocktails CAD 15

- **Best Time:** Weekend brunch (reserve two weeks ahead)

- **Why Try It:** Upscale vegan Asian fusion feels indulgent. I brought my mom for brunch and even she forgot it was egg-free. The "Lychee Martini" was a highlight.

- **Additional Info:** Gluten-free and nut-free options available. They sell vegan pantry items like mayo and plant-based bacon.

Practical Tips

Use the HappyCow app to find veg and vegan spots. For pastries, try Hibiscus Cafe (71 Bathurst St) where treats run CAD 4–6. Grocery hunt at St. Lawrence Market's north hall for vegan cheeses and specialty tofu. If you're in town during Vegandale Festival, tickets start at CAD 30 and include unlimited tastings. For quick eats, the jackfruit taco cart at Trinity Bellwoods Park serves tacos for CAD 8 on weekends. Many restaurants offer weekday lunch specials—look for prix fixe menus (around CAD 28) at Planta. Follow local vegan bloggers for pop-up events and food-truck schedules. With these tips, plant-based eating in Toronto is simple and tasty.

Coffee Culture and Independent Cafés

Toronto takes coffee seriously. Baristas here treat coffee like craft beer—adjusting roast levels and trying beans from different regions. You'll find cafés roasting in-house, offering single-origin pour-overs, and hosting community events. Whether you need a strong espresso before a museum visit or a quiet spot to work, there's a café for you. I spent my first week hopping between spots, sampling brews and talking to roasters. Below are two favorites and tips for exploring further.

Sam James Coffee Bar

- **Where:** Flagship at 297 College St (multiple locations)
- **Price:** CAD 3.50–5 for espresso drinks; beans CAD 18/12 oz bag
- **Best Time:** Weekday mornings (8 AM–10 AM)
- **Why Try It:** They roast in-house and offer blends like "Sam's Blend," which I now order by the bag. The espresso has consistent flavor and body.
- **Additional Info:** Seating is limited to bar stools and a small communal table. They sell pour-over gear and offer subscription bags on their website.

Jimmy's Coffee

- **Where:** 215 Spadina Ave (and others)
- **Price:** CAD 4–6 for specialty lattes; lavender latte CAD 6.50
- **Best Time:** Mid-afternoon (2 PM–4 PM)
- **Why Try It:** Their lavender latte is a local favorite. I spent an afternoon here working on my blog, and the barista recommended a bright Ethiopia roast that became my go-to.
- **Additional Info:** Outlets and communal tables make it good for remote work. They host coffee cupping events (CAD 20) to learn tasting notes.

Exploring More

Check out Pilot Coffee Roasters at 1201 Queen St. W—
pour-overs start at CAD 5. Dineen Coffee Co (140 Yonge St)
offers espresso for CAD 4–6 in a spacious setting. The Toronto
Coffee Festival each fall (tickets CAD 25) features over 50
vendors and tastings. Weekend pop-ups at Evergreen Brick
Works serve lattes for CAD 4. To find hidden gems, search
Instagram hashtags like #TorontoCoffee and follow barista
competitions. Many roasters offer subscription discounts if you
buy beans monthly.

Practical Tips

Bring your own mug for a CAD 0.50 discount. Most cafés accept card and mobile pay, but small spots may be contactless only. If you need Wi-Fi, look for "Work Here" signs or ask staff. For hands-on learning, George Brown College offers a barista course (CAD 400 for a one-day class). Follow cafés on social media for daily brew updates and pop-up events. With these tips, you'll find Toronto's coffee scene welcoming and full of flavor.

Top Brunch & Late-Night Eats

In Toronto, brunch lines stretch around the block, and late-night diners stay open until the early hours. Brunch menus mix sweet and savory—think pancakes with lemon ricotta or eggs Benedict with house-made sausage. After dark, diners serve comfort food like burgers and poutine to crowds spilling in from bars. I waited an hour for brunch and later ducked into a 24-hour spot at 2 AM, discovering that Toronto's food scene truly never sleeps. Below are two must-visit places: Mildred's Temple Kitchen for brunch and The Senator for late-night comfort.

Mildred's Temple Kitchen

- **Where:** 85 Hanna Ave, Liberty Village
- **Price:** CAD 18–24 for entrées; bottomless mimosas CAD 15
- **Best Time:** Weekends at 10 AM opening (arrive 10–15 minutes early)
- **Why Try It:** Their blueberry buttermilk pancakes are legendary—light, fluffy, and packed with berries. On my first visit, the stack disappeared in minutes.
- **Additional Info:** Reservations for parties of six or more. Weekday market counter offers pastries and coffee (CAD 4) for grab-and-go.

The Senator

- **Where:** 249 Victoria St

- **Price:** CAD 8–14 for breakfast plates; smoked meat sandwich CAD 12

- **Best Time:** After 11 PM on Fridays/Saturdays

- **Why Try It:** Open since 1929, this diner serves eggs and bacon at 3 AM. I stumbled in after a concert and found their smoked meat sandwich cured my late-night hunger better than any snack.

- **Additional Info:** Cash only; ATM nearby. Counter seating and back booths. Don't miss the apple pie (CAD 6) for dessert.

Practical Tips

To avoid brunch waits, try weekday lunches or smaller spots like Aunties & Uncles (110 Ossington Ave) where breakfast sandwiches run CAD 6. For late-night shawarma, check food trucks near King & Spadina open until 4 AM. Use Uber Eats or DoorDash for delivery if you can't leave your hotel. Wear layers—brunch lines can form outside, and diners stay open in all weather. With these spots and tips, you'll be ready to brunch and munch around the clock in Toronto.

Craft Beer, Distilleries & Cocktail Bars

Toronto's drink scene has something for every taste. Craft breweries in converted warehouses serve hazy IPAs and fruited sours. Distilleries in the historic Distillery District turn local grains into rye whiskey and gin. Cocktail bars use creative techniques—smoke, foams, and custom glassware—to make every drink an experience. On a recent weekend, I spent an afternoon at a brewery and ended the night sipping smoked-herb cocktails. Below are three standout spots and tips for enjoying them.

Bellwoods Brewery

- **Where:** 124 Ossington Ave
- **Price:** CAD 7–9 per pint; flights CAD 12–15
- **Best Time:** Weekends noon–4 PM (patio open, live music)
- **Why Try It:** Their "Jelly King" sour tastes like summer fruit—bright, tart, and refreshing. I shared a flight with friends and discovered new favorites.
- **Additional Info:** Limited releases drop Friday mornings; follow their Instagram and arrive early. Taproom is cashless and family-friendly until 6 PM.

Spirit of York Distillery

- **Where:** 34 Distillery Lane, Distillery District
- **Price:** Tours CAD 20 (includes four tastings); cocktails CAD 10–15
- **Best Time:** Afternoon tours at 4 PM (bar opens right after)
- **Why Try It:** Their Canadian rye whiskey has subtle maple notes. On my tour, the guide explained the aging process, and the samples showed real depth.
- **Additional Info:** Gift shop sells small-batch bottles (CAD 55). Take the 504 King streetcar or ride-share— parking in the district is limited.

BarChef

- **Where:** 472 Queen St. W
- **Price:** CAD 15–18 per cocktail
- **Best Time:** Weekday evenings (6–8 PM) for a quieter vibe

- **Why Try It:** Their cocktails come with smoke and theatrical flair. I ordered the "Smoked Rosemary" and watched the bartender light fresh rosemary at my table.

- **Additional Info:** Reservations recommended for groups over four. Cashless only; dress code is smart casual. No food served—plan to eat beforehand.

Practical Tips

Book brewery and distillery tours online in advance, especially on weekends. For a crawl, head to Dundas West—Henderson Brewing (1286 Dundas St. W) and Brasserie T! (1085 Dupont St) are close by. Toronto Cocktail Festival in June (tickets CAD 50) features dozens of bars and tastings. Always drink responsibly—use ride-share apps or a designated driver. If you buy cans to go, remember the CAD 0.10 deposit per can. With these spots and tips, you'll experience Toronto's spirited side from hops to herbs.

Chapter 7: Neighborhood Walks & Urban Life

Kensington Market

Kensington Market feels like stepping into someone's colorful living room—streets lined with murals, vintage shops, and food stalls all vying for your attention. I remember my first Saturday there: I sipped a mango-ginger juice from a sidewalk cart, struck up a conversation with the vendor about the best empanada spot in town, and ended up wandering for hours, sampling tacos and hunting for vinyl records.

Quick Facts

- **Address:** Bounded by College St (north), Dundas St W (south), Bathurst St (west), Spadina Ave (east)

- **Price:** Free to explore; budget $15–$25 for snacks, coffee, and small finds

- **Activities:** Vintage shopping, street art spotting, global street food, weekend farmers' market

- **How to get there:** 505 Dundas or 506 Carlton streetcar to Spadina Ave, then walk one block west

- **Best time to visit:** Late spring through early fall; Saturday mornings for pedestrian-only market

- **Why visit:** Toronto's original melting pot—an open-air showcase of creativity, food, and culture

- **Additional info:** Many vendors are cash-only; ATMs can charge fees

Kensington's narrow lanes are pedestrian-only on weekends, so it's easy to drift from one colorful storefront to the next without worrying about cars. Start on Augusta Avenue, where murals stretch the length of building walls. Pop into **Globe Textiles** for hand-printed T-shirts (around $25 each), then duck next door to **Sonic Boom** to flip through vinyl—reggae, jazz, '90s alt-rock— you'll find it all for $20–$30 a record.

When hunger strikes, follow the aromas. The taco stall **Seven Lives** serves Baja-style fish tacos for about $5 apiece. Don't miss the jerk chicken at **Rasta Pasta** (~$12), or the vegan samosas at **Mango Cheeks** (~$2 each). If you're there on Saturday morning, the small farmers' market sets up on Kensington Avenue—fresh microgreens, homemade bread, and seasonal produce at very reasonable prices.

Practical tip: wear comfortable shoes. The cobblestones can be uneven, and you'll want to wander. Keep small bills handy— many food carts and vintage vendors don't accept cards. If you're hunting a specific item—say, antique postcards—ask around; locals and shopkeepers are friendly and love pointing out hidden stalls.

Photography lovers, bring a wide-angle lens. Every corner has a photo-worthy scene: a spray-painted mural of Frida Kahlo, a rainbow-painted telephone booth, or a bicycle wrapped in fairy lights. If you want a guided experience, several local walking-tour companies offer two-hour "market deep-dives" for about $25 per person—great for background on the neighborhood's bohemian roots.

Kensington's energy changes from day to night. By evening, the lanterns strung above the lanes glow, and some bars—like **Bellwoods Brewery** off Dundas—open up with local craft beers ($6–$8 a pint) and occasional live music. It's a perfect way to cap off a day of wandering. Whether you're on a tight budget or ready to splurge on a one-of-a-kind vintage jacket, Kensington Market is a must-visit slice of Toronto that feels both familiar and endlessly surprising.

Queen Street West

Queen Street West is Toronto's trend laboratory. Boutiques, galleries, and bars line the street, each competing for your attention. On an unplanned Tuesday afternoon, I ducked into a pop-up gallery showcasing local photographers, ended up chatting with the curator, and walked away with a framed print of the city skyline.

Quick Facts

- **Address:** Queen St W from University Ave to Dufferin St
- **Price:** Free to stroll; gallery entry $5–$15; coffee or craft beer $4–$8
- **Activities:** Boutique shopping, art gallery hopping, live music at The Drake Hotel, street art photography
- **How to get there:** 501 Queen streetcar; hop off at Spadina, Portland, or Bathurst
- **Best time to visit:** Weekday afternoons for a quieter experience; Friday/Saturday evenings for nightlife
- **Why visit:** Cutting-edge fashion, indie art, and live music all in one corridor
- **Additional info:** Side streets and alleys often host unannounced pop-ups

Begin at **Spadina and Queen**, where the **Museum of Contemporary Canadian Art (MOCA)** Design Store offers locally made home goods and prints for $20–$50. A block west, **Blue Ruby** stocks hand-crafted jewelry—bracelets and rings from $30–$80. Keep an eye out for laneway galleries like **CLARK**, where exhibitions change monthly and admission is usually $10 or free on first Fridays.

Food options are equally creative. Grab a matcha latte at **Dark Horse Espresso** ($4) and a slice of sour-dough pizza at **Pizzeria**

Libretto (~$6). For a sweet treat, **Fugo Desserts** serves mochi ice cream and Japanese-style crepes for $5–$8.

Live music fans should head to **The Drake Hotel** (1150 Queen St W). The underground lounge hosts local bands most nights, with no cover charge or $10 door fee on weekends. If comedy is more your speed, **The Second City** (51 Mercer St) sits just north—tickets run $25–$40, and the improv shows are always fresh.

Pro tip: wander side streets like **Cumberland** and **Baldwin** for hidden cafés and thrift shops. You might stumble on a private gallery opening or a speakeasy-style bar. If you're hunting street art, look up—many murals occupy entire building sides.

Queen West is also home to **Graffiti Alley**, between Spadina and Portland. It's a free, open-air art gallery where every inch of brick is covered in color. Visit mid-morning for soft light and fewer people.

Queen Street West changes by season. In summer, patios spill onto sidewalks, and the street hums with outdoor DJs. In winter, shop windows glow with festive displays, and you can warm up in one of the many heated cafés. No matter when you go, Queen West feels alive—a place to see and be seen, to discover the next big thing in Toronto's art and fashion scenes.

The Annex & Bloor Street Culture Corridor

The Annex is where you'll find students, book lovers, and comedy fans all in one neighborhood. One afternoon, I wandered into **Type Books**, grabbed a latte for $4, and lost track of time in the fiction section. Later, I caught an improv show at **Second City**, laughing so hard my sides ached.

Quick Facts

- **Address:** Bloor St W from Spadina Ave to Bathurst St, plus adjacent side streets
- **Price:** Free to wander; bookstore coffee $3–$5; Second City tickets $25–$40; Bata Shoe Museum entry $16
- **Activities:** Independent bookstores, campus strolls, improv comedy, museum visits
- **How to get there:** Bloor-Danforth subway line to Spadina or Bathurst station
- **Best time to visit:** Late afternoon (2–5 pm) when shops are open and campus paths are quiet
- **Why visit:** A blend of academic energy, literary hangouts, and performance art
- **Additional info:** The University of Toronto campus is a short walk north

Start at **Book City** (348 Bloor St W), one of Toronto's largest indie bookstores. You can spend an hour browsing poetry, history, or graphic novels—most paperbacks run $15–$25. Next door, **Café Landwer** offers shakshuka for $14 and excellent espresso.

Walk east along Bloor to the **Bata Shoe Museum** (327 Bloor St W). For $16, you'll see shoes from ancient Egypt to modern couture. The museum's small café serves tea and scones if you need a break.

Cross to the north side of Bloor and follow Philosopher's Walk through U of T's leafy campus. The path leads past sandstone buildings and quiet courtyards—perfect for a midday stroll.

When evening falls, head to **Second City** (51 Mercer St) for improv. Shows run nightly at 7 pm and 9:30 pm; buy tickets online in advance to snag seats for $25–$40. After the show, grab a late snack at **Roti** (90 Harbord St), where you can build-your-own roti wrap for about S12.

If you're here in spring, check out the **Harbord Street Festival** (late May). Local artists set up booths, live bands play on makeshift stages, and food trucks line the street. It's free to attend, though you might want $20–$30 for snacks and small purchases.

Practical tip: parking is limited and expensive (up to $5/hour). Take the subway or rent a bike via Bike Share Toronto; there are stations at both Spadina and Bathurst.

The Annex feels like a cozy village in the city. Between the smell of fresh coffee, the hush of library halls, and the roar of laughter at Second City, it captures Toronto's love of learning and its playful side. Whether you're hunting a rare book or just looking for a relaxed afternoon, this corridor has something for everyone.

Leslieville & Riverside

East of downtown, Leslieville and Riverside feel like a small town planted in the city. I once queued for 45 minutes outside **Lady Marmalade** for their eggs Benedict on sweet-potato hash—totally worth the wait.

Quick Facts

- **Address:** Queen St E from Broadview Ave to Jones Ave; Riverside extends north to Gerrard St

- **Price:** Free to explore; brunch $15–$25; craft beer $6–$8

- **Activities:** Brunch spots, antique shops, craft breweries, film-location walks

- **How to get there:** 504 King streetcar to Broadview, then walk east; or 506 Carlton to Queen & Logan

- **Best time to visit:** Weekend mornings for brunch; weekday evenings for quieter bars

- **Why visit:** Laid-back vibe, family-friendly, and full of hidden cafés

- **Additional info:** Street parking is scarce—use transit or bike

Begin at **Lady Marmalade** (908 Queen St E). Their eggs Benedict on sweet-potato hash ($18) draws locals and visitors alike. If the line is long, head next door to **Café Neon** for avocado toast ($12) and cold brew ($4).

Wander east and pop into **Leslieville Flea** on Saturdays—local artisans sell crafts, vintage clothes, and homemade treats. Budget $10–$30 for small finds.

For beer lovers, **Riverside Brewing Co.** (60 Colgate Ave) offers pints of their flagship pale ale for $6. The taproom is casual, with picnic tables and occasional live music.

Film buffs can follow a self-guided **Scott Pilgrim vs. the World** walking tour. Many scenes were shot along Queen St E; pick up a free map from **Hello City** café (1066 Queen St E).

If you want a quiet break, cross the Don River via the Queen St bridge and walk north along the **Don Valley Trail**. It's a green ribbon through the city, perfect for a 30-minute stroll or quick jog.

Leslieville's evenings are mellow. **The Broadview Hotel** (106 Broadview Ave) has a rooftop bar with skyline views—cocktails start at $12. If you're craving comfort food, **Leslie's** (1298 Queen St E) serves gourmet grilled cheese sandwiches for $10–$14.

Pro tip: many cafés offer free Wi-Fi and power outlets—great if you need to catch up on emails. If you're visiting in summer, keep an eye out for outdoor movie nights in **Withrow Park**, just a few blocks north of Queen.

Leslieville and Riverside capture Toronto's friendly side. You'll see families walking dogs, hipsters with laptops, and retirees chatting on benches. It's the kind of place where strangers say hello—and you might just leave with a new favorite brunch spot.

Liberty Village

Once an industrial area of brick warehouses, Liberty Village now hums with tech startups, loft apartments, and fitness studios. During a week I spent working nearby, my morning routine was the same: a flat white at **Boxcar Social**, then a walk through June Callwood Park before settling in at a communal table.

Quick Facts

- **Address:** Strachan Ave (east), Dufferin St (west), King St W (north), Liberty St (south)
- **Price:** Free to wander; coffee $4–$6; yoga classes $15–$25; craft beer $6–$8
- **Activities:** Park strolls, boutique shopping, yoga, craft breweries, weekend market
- **How to get there:** 504 King streetcar to Strachan; GO train to Exhibition, then 10-minute walk
- **Best time to visit:** Weekday mornings for calm; Thursday/Friday evenings for happy hours
- **Why visit:** A model of urban renewal—green spaces amid creative offices and cafés
- **Additional info:** Small weekend farmers' market on Jefferson Ave (Saturdays, 9 am–2 pm)

Start your visit at **June Callwood Park**, a small green space with benches, a fountain, and a dog-friendly lawn. It's ideal for a quick stretch or people-watching.

Coffee lovers will gravitate to **Boxcar Social** (33 Hanna Ave). Their single-origin pour-overs ($5) and fresh pastries ($3–$5) fuel many local freelancers. Next door, **Union Chicken** offers fried-chicken sandwiches for $12.

Fitness fans can drop into **Power Yoga Canada** (55 Stewart St) for a $20 drop-in class. The studio overlooks the park, so you can cool down with a stretch on the grass afterward.

Afternoons are perfect for boutique browsing. **Local Licks** (37 Hanna Ave) stocks handcrafted jewelry, while **Mabel's Fables** (10 Hanna Ave) carries children's books and toys if you're traveling with little ones.

When you're ready for a drink, head to **Craft & Commerce** (53 Abell St). Their rotating list of local beers ($6–$8) and craft cocktails ($12–$14) pair nicely with bar snacks like poutine or charcuterie boards.

If you're here on a Saturday, walk south to **Jefferson Ave** for the small but well-curated Liberty Village Farmers' Market. You'll find fresh produce, baked goods, and handmade soaps. Plan on $20–$30 if you want to take home a mix of treats.

Practical tip: parking can be pricey ($4–$6/hour). If you're driving, look for street parking on nearby residential streets. Otherwise, take the streetcar or GO train—there's a Bike Share Toronto station at Exhibition GO if you want to pedal around

The Beaches

Stretching along Lake Ontario's shoreline, The Beaches feels like a seaside town tucked into the city. On my first visit, I took an evening stroll along the boardwalk, letting the water lap at my ankles as joggers and families passed by—pure relaxation.

Quick Facts

- **Address:** Queen St E to the lake, between Coxwell Ave and Victoria Park Ave

- **Price:** Free; bike rentals $10–$15/hour; ice cream $3–$5; beach volleyball $5/hour

- **Activities:** Boardwalk walks, swimming, volleyball, bike rides, ice cream stops

- **How to get there:** 501 Queen streetcar to Woodbine Ave, then south; or 92 Woodbine bus

- **Best time to visit:** Late May through early September; early mornings or evenings for fewer crowds

- **Why visit:** Sandy shores, friendly vibe, and a genuine small-town feel within the city

- **Additional info:** Lifeguards on duty June–August; public restrooms at main beach entrances

Start at **Woodbine Beach**, where you'll find a wide stretch of sand, volleyball nets ($5/hour), and lifeguards from 10 am–6 pm. Bring your own ball or rent one on-site for $3.

Next, follow the 4 km **boardwalk** east toward **Kew Gardens**. The path is flat and paved—ideal for walking, jogging, or biking (rentals $10/hour). You'll pass children building sandcastles, dog-owners on morning walks, and local musicians strumming guitars.

Around halfway, stop at the iconic **Beaches Ice Cream** (2142 Queen St E) for a soft-serve cone ($3–$5). The pastel-pink building is a local landmark—don't miss the vintage signage.

If you're here on a Sunday, head to the small farmers' market in **Kew Gardens** (10 am–2 pm). You'll find fresh bread, honey, and handmade crafts—plan $20 if you want a decent haul.

For a change of pace, explore the quiet streets north of Queen. The houses here range from quaint cottages to grand Victorians. It's a peaceful contrast to the buzz of the boardwalk.

Practical tip: sunscreen and water are must-haves in summer. Shade is limited along the beach. If you're visiting in July or August, arrive before 10 am or after 6 pm to avoid peak crowds.

By late afternoon, the water reflects the sky in shades of orange and pink. It's the perfect backdrop for photos or simply sitting on a bench and watching sailboats drift by. As the sun dips, families pack up picnic blankets and local cafés like **Balmy Beach Club** open their patios for dinner.

The Beaches is where Torontonians come to unwind. You'll find no skyscrapers, just the lake, the sand, and a laid-back spirit that reminds you how lucky this city is to have its own slice of waterfront paradise.

Harbourfront & Waterfront Trail

Toronto's waterfront is the city's front porch—a mix of culture, recreation, and skyline views. Last summer, I rented a kayak at Harbourfront Canoe & Kayak Centre and paddled beneath the CN Tower as the sun set, painting the water gold.

Quick Facts

- **Address:** Queen's Quay W from Bathurst St to Yonge St; Waterfront Trail extends beyond the city
- **Price:** Free to stroll; bike or kayak rentals $20–$40/hour; Harbourfront Centre events $0–$20
- **Activities:** Walking, biking, kayaking, art galleries, outdoor concerts, boat cruises
- **How to get there:** 509 Harbourfront streetcar to Lower Simcoe; Union Station is a 10-minute walk
- **Best time to visit:** May–October; mornings for quiet, evenings for dining and events
- **Why visit:** A dynamic mix of outdoor fun, arts, and stunning city-meets-lake scenery
- **Additional info:** In winter, the Natrel Rink offers lakeside skating (rentals $8)

Begin at **Harbourfront Centre** (235 Queens Quay W). Check their website for free or low-cost events—summer brings outdoor concerts, film screenings, and dance performances. Many are drop-in and family-friendly.

If you want to be on the water, head to **Harbourfront Canoe & Kayak Centre** (65 Queens Quay W). Single kayaks rent for $20/hour; stand-up paddleboards are $25/hour. No experience needed—they offer quick safety demos.

For a land-based ride, grab a bike from **Bike Share Toronto**. The Waterfront Trail runs east toward the Beaches and west toward Humber Bay. It's mostly flat and well-marked—perfect for a 10 km ride.

Art lovers should stop at the **Power Plant Contemporary Art Gallery** (231 Queens Quay W). Admission is free; rotating exhibits showcase Canadian and international artists.

As evening approaches, stroll toward **Rees Street Pier** for skyline views at sunset. The long wooden pier juts into the lake—great for photos. Nearby, **Cabana Pool Bar** (11 Polson St) hosts rooftop DJs and cocktails ($12–$15) in summer.

If you prefer boats, **Toronto Harbour Tours** runs 45-minute sightseeing cruises for $30. They depart from Queen's Quay every hour and offer commentary on landmarks like the Toronto Islands and the old ferry docks.

Practical tip: wear layers. The breeze off Lake Ontario can be cool, even in summer evenings. Sunscreen is also important—there's little shade along the trail.

In winter, the **Natrel Rink** (207 Queens Quay W) opens for skating. Rentals are $8, and the rink overlooks the lake and city lights—magical after dark.

The Harbourfront and Waterfront Trail capture Toronto's best qualities: accessible outdoor space, cultural events, and stunning views. Whether you're paddling, biking, or simply watching the sun sink behind the skyline, this stretch of the city reminds you that Toronto truly is defined by its water.

High Park

Address: 1873 Bloor St W, Toronto, ON M6R 2Z3
Price: Free entry; small fees may apply for zoo or special events.
Activities/Things to Do: Walking and jogging trails, cherry-blossom viewing, picnicking, playgrounds, splash pad, High Park Zoo, birdwatching, cycling.
How to Get There:

- **Subway:** Line 2 to High Park Station (north entrance).

- **Streetcar:** 506 Carlton to Howard Park Ave.

- **Bike:** Follow Martin Goodman Trail then city bike lanes west.
  Best Time to Visit:

- **Late April:** Peak cherry-blossom bloom.

- **October:** Peak fall foliage.
  Why You Should Visit: It's a 400-acre green oasis minutes from downtown, with trails, wildlife, playgrounds, seasonal events, and a free zoo.
  Additional Info:

- Parking at High Park Loop ($3–5/hr).

- Guided nature walks on weekends—check the City of Toronto site.

- Dogs must be on leash except in the off-leash area south of Bloor.

High Park feels like a small wilderness tucked into the city. The main paths wind under maple and oak trees, opening onto lawns where families picnic and students study. On a late-afternoon walk last summer, I spotted a red-tailed hawk perched atop a lamp post, scanning the grass for squirrels.

In spring, over 1,600 cherry trees line the West Road and the pond's edge. Hanami-style picnics are popular—locals spread blankets under pink blossoms. To avoid crowds, I arrived at 8 AM on a weekday, grabbed a bench by Grenadier Pond, and watched the petals drift onto the water. A coffee and croissant from the nearby café made it a perfect morning.

Kids love the Jamie Bell Adventure Playground with its rope bridges and slides. Next door, the splash pad offers a safe way to cool off—bring water shoes, as the surface can be slippery. Further south, the free High Park Zoo houses llamas, bison, capybaras, and wallabies. The zoo closes earlier in winter, so check posted hours.

Cyclists can enter via the west gate, linking to the Martin Goodman Trail. Bike racks stand near the playgrounds and zoo. One Saturday, I rented a bike, pedaled through the park, and stopped at a food truck near the south end for ice cream. Lines form after noon—arrive early for the best flavors.

Picnic tables and barbecue pits near the northeast entrance are first-come, first-served. I once shared a table with a group from Montreal, trading poutine for their grilled sausages. For a quieter spot, head deeper into the woods; small clearings offer space for blankets and baskets.

Seasonal events add variety. From June to August, the park's amphitheater hosts free Shakespeare performances—arrive an hour early to claim a grassy spot. In winter, a small rink near Colborne Lodge opens for skating; skate rentals run about CA$5.

Facilities include restrooms at the north entrance, playground, and zoo. Water fountains dot the park, but carrying a refillable bottle is wise. Accessible paths suitable for wheelchairs and strollers run along the north side; beyond that, trails can be uneven or muddy after rain—sturdy shoes are a must.

Chapter 8: Outdoor Adventures & Nature Escapes

Don Valley Trails & Evergreen Brick Works

Address: Evergreen Brick Works, 550 Bayview Ave, Toronto, ON M4W 3X8

Price: Free entry; farmers' market and workshops have separate fees.

Activities/Things to Do: Hiking, mountain biking, farmers' market, guided nature tours, outdoor skating, cross-country skiing, art exhibits, birdwatching.

How to Get There:

- **Subway + Bus:** Line 2 to Broadview Station, then TTC bus 28 to Bayview & Pottery Rd.

- **Bike:** Follow Bayview Ave bike lanes north; bike racks onsite.

- **Car:** Limited parking; nearby street parking if full.
  Best Time to Visit:

- **Spring–Fall:** Trails are green and dry.

- **Winter:** Outdoor rink and ski trails open December–March.
  Why You Should Visit: It blends an industrial past with nature, offering year-round activities from markets to winter sports.
  Additional Info:

- Farmers' market Saturdays, 8 AM–1 PM.

- Check Evergreen's website for workshops and guided walks.
- Dress in layers—valley temperatures can be cooler.

Evergreen Brick Works sits in the Don Valley ravine, where an old brick factory has been reborn as a community hub. The plaza features restored kilns and galleries. Behind it, trails climb and dip along the Don River. On a misty May morning, I followed the red-blazed trail and quickly left traffic noise behind. Birds sang overhead, and small waterfalls appeared around bends.

The Saturday market fills the plaza with local vendors selling honey, baked goods, and crafts. I once arrived early, snagged a loaf of rye bread still warm, and watched chefs inspect heirloom tomatoes. For a quieter visit, come before 9 AM or on a weekday.

Bike rentals run spring through fall. You can choose a standard or fat-tire bike for rougher trails. Cycling north, I passed wetlands where herons fished. Helmets are mandatory, and trails can be muddy—fenders and good tires help.

In winter, the ice rink opens for free skating (CA$5 skate rental). Nearby, groomed ski trails wind through bare trees. One January, I joined a small ski group under gray skies, the valley's quiet a sharp contrast to the city.

Inside the factory, art exhibits focus on sustainability. I took a flower-arranging workshop using local blooms. The instructor shared tips on conditioning branches and extending vase life. A café serves soup, sandwiches, and coffee—perfect after a chilly hike.

Restrooms and changing areas are in the main building. Benches and picnic tables dot the plaza. Street parking along Bayview Ave is limited; transit or bike is easier.

Guided nature walks run weekends, covering birdwatching, native plants, and river ecology. They last about two hours and are free (donations welcome).

Toronto Islands Kayaking & Biking

Address: Jack Layton Ferry Terminal, 9 Queens Quay W, Toronto, ON M5J 2H3

Price:

- **Ferry:** CA$8.19 round-trip (adult), CA$5.54 (child 2–12)

- **Kayak Rental:** ~CA$20/hour

- **Bike Rental:** ~CA$8–10/hour
  Activities/Things to Do: Kayaking, cycling, beach swimming, picnics, Centreville Amusement Park, lighthouse visits, birdwatching.
  How to Get There:

- **Subway:** Line 1 to Union Station, then 10-minute walk east.

- **Bike/Walk:** Waterfront Trail leads directly to terminal.

- **Car:** Nearby parking garages, but transit is easier.
  Best Time to Visit: May–September, when rentals and ferry service are in full swing.
  Why You Should Visit: A quick ferry ride delivers you to car-free islands with beaches, trails, and skyline views.
  Additional Info:

- Ferry runs every 15–30 minutes; check online.

- Rentals are first-come, first-served—arrive early on weekends.

- Pack water, snacks, and sun protection; shade is limited.

A five-minute ferry ride from downtown, the Toronto Islands feel a world away. On a July morning, I boarded at 9 AM and watched the CN Tower fade behind us. At Centre Island, bike and kayak rentals line the docks. Kayaks cost about CA$20/hr with life jackets included. I paddled west toward Gibraltar Point Lighthouse, keeping my distance from swimmers and other boats. The calm water makes it ideal for beginners.

Cycling is another draw. Bike rentals are around CA$8/hr. Paths loop around Centre Island, Ward's Island, and Hanlan's Point. On a crisp September afternoon, I pedaled past picnic areas filled with families tossing frisbees. The flat terrain and clear signs make navigation easy.

Beaches include Centre Island Beach (with washrooms and change rooms), Hanlan's Point Beach (quieter, with a clothing-optional section), and Gibraltar Point Beach. Water shoes help if you plan to wade—the lake bottom can be rocky.

Centreville Amusement Park offers kid-friendly rides, mini-golf, and a petting zoo. Admission is CA$11; rides cost extra. Food stands sell hot dogs and ice cream—bring snacks if you're on a budget.

Picnic tables and grills dot the islands. One trip, I packed sandwiches and found a shaded spot on Ward's Island. Remember to carry out your trash; bins sit near docks.

Restrooms at Centre Island docks and beach entrances are available, but fountains are limited—bring a refillable bottle. No lifeguards patrol the beaches; swim at your own risk.

The ferry schedule changes by season. In summer, service runs early to late; in spring and fall, hours shorten. Check the official site before you go.

Bluffer's Park & Scarborough Bluffs

Address: 1 Brimley Rd S, Scarborough, ON M1M 3W3
Price: Free entry; parking CA$5–10 (seasonal).
Activities/Things to Do: Hiking cliff-top trails, beach visits, picnicking, kayaking, fishing, photography.
How to Get There:

- **GO Train + Bus:** Lakeshore East to Guildwood Station, then TTC bus 57 to Brimley & Kingston.

- **Car:** Parking lot near beach entrance (fee applies). **Best Time to Visit:**

- **Summer (June–September):** Beach and shaded hikes.

- **Fall (October):** Quiet trails and colorful leaves. **Why You Should Visit:** Dramatic limestone cliffs and lake views make it one of Toronto's most striking landscapes. **Additional Info:**

- Trails can be unstable—stay on marked paths.

- Facilities open seasonally; check Parks Toronto for hours.

- No lifeguard on beach; swim with caution.

The Scarborough Bluffs rise up to 90 m above Lake Ontario, but Bluffer's Park gives the easiest access. From the parking lot, a sandy beach stretches along the water, backed by towering cliffs. On a clear afternoon, I hiked the cliff-top trail east, stopping at wooden lookout platforms to photograph the multi-colored layers.

The beach area has picnic tables and charcoal grills—first-come, first-served. I arrived at 10 AM on a hot July Saturday, grabbed a shaded table, and grilled hot dogs and corn. Bring your own charcoal and tools; rentals aren't available.

The cliff-top trail runs east and west for about 2 km. It's mostly flat but narrows in spots. After rain, the path gets slippery, so wear sturdy shoes. I once slipped on wet clay and was glad for my hiking boots. Rail-fenced lookout points offer safe photo spots.

Kayaking from the beach is another option. Rentals run about CA$25/hr. Paddle close to the cliffs—watch for submerged rocks. On one trip, I saw a great blue heron perched on a ledge and a school of small fish near the shore.

Fishing is popular off the pier and shore. An Ontario fishing license is required. Bass and perch are common catches. I once landed a small bass on my second cast—an unexpected bonus.

Washrooms near the parking lot open from June to September. A small snack kiosk sells cold drinks and ice cream at beach level. Prices are higher than town, so bring water and snacks if you prefer.

Public transit takes about an hour from downtown. If you drive, arrive before 11 AM on weekends to find a spot. After 2 PM, the lot often fills up.

Humber River Recreational Trail

Address (Trailhead): Old Mill Station, 65 Old Mill Rd, Toronto, ON M8X 1G5
Price: Free
Activities/Things to Do: Walking, running, cycling, picnicking, canoeing, kayaking, snowshoeing, cross-country skiing, birdwatching.
How to Get There:

- **Subway:** Line 2 to Old Mill Station; trail entrance just south.

- **Bike:** Connect via Martin Goodman Trail along Lake Ontario.

- **Car:** Street parking near Old Mill.
  Best Time to Visit:

- **Spring–Fall (April–October):** Trails clear and green.

- **Winter (December–March):** Snowshoeing and skiing on groomed sections.
  Why You Should Visit: A peaceful riverside route with parks, historic bridges, and wildlife, all within city limits.
  Additional Info:

- Some sections are gravel—mountain or hybrid bikes work best.

- Facilities are limited—carry water and snacks.

- Canoe clubs offer rentals and lessons in spring.

The Humber River trail follows the river from the northwest suburbs to Lake Ontario. Starting at Old Mill Station, a paved path runs alongside the water, passing under century-old bridges and through wooded parks. On a June morning, I hopped off the subway, clipped on my helmet, and joined runners and cyclists heading north.

The first few kilometers are flat and paved—ideal for families. Benches line the path, offering river views. At Kings Mill Park, the trail opens onto lawns and picnic tables. I once stopped there for a lunch of sandwiches and fruit, listening to rapids over small rock ledges.

North of Lambton Woods, the surface turns to packed gravel and winds through a tree canopy. After rain, it gets muddy—fenders and sturdy shoes help. Look for small waterfalls cascading over rocks in spring. I slipped once on wet clay and was glad for my hiking boots.

Canoe clubs have docks along the river. In May, I joined a beginner canoe lesson. They provided paddles and life jackets, teaching strokes before we paddled past willows and nesting ducks. Check club websites for rentals and schedules.

In winter, groomed ski and snowshoe trails open through Lambton Woods. On a snowy January day, I strapped on snowshoes and followed tracks left by earlier hikers. The quiet, white landscape felt miles from the city.

Birdwatchers spot herons, kingfishers, and occasionally bald eagles near Humber Marshes. Bring binoculars and scan the water's edge. I once watched a great blue heron stand motionless for minutes before striking at fish.

Restrooms are at Old Mill and Kings Mill Park; beyond that, facilities are scarce. Carry water and snacks for longer rides. Trail maps are posted at entrances; an offline map helps avoid wrong turns.

The trail links to the Claireville Trail northwest and the Martin Goodman Trail south, letting you plan full-day rides. On a recent weekend, I rode from Old Mill to the waterfront and back—about 40 km total with breaks.

Toronto Botanical Garden

Address: 777 Lawrence Ave E, North York, ON M3C 1P2
Price:

- Adults: CA$10
- Seniors: CA$8
- Students: CA$5
- Children under 5: Free
- Members: Free year-round
  Activities/Things to Do: Garden tours, themed walks, workshops (flower arranging, composting), photography, children's garden, Tea Garden Café.
  How to Get There:
- **Subway + Bus:** Line 1 to Lawrence Station, then TTC bus 34 to Leslie & Lawrence.
- **Car:** Onsite parking available.
  Best Time to Visit:
- **Late Spring–Early Fall (May–September):** Peak blooms.
- **Winter:** Outdoor art installations and holiday light displays.
  Why You Should Visit: Seventeen themed demonstration gardens showcase plants suited to Toronto's climate, plus hands-on programs.
  Additional Info:
- Tripods allowed weekdays; weekend use limited.
- Check website for "Garden Lights" evening events.
- Café seating is mostly outdoors; indoor space is limited.

The Toronto Botanical Garden is an eight-acre oasis of demonstration gardens designed to inspire home gardeners and delight visitors. As you enter, you'll see the water garden with floating lilies framed by a wooden pergola. On a sunny May afternoon, I joined a guided tour led by a volunteer who explained how native plants support local wildlife.

Each themed garden highlights different plants. In the fragrance garden, roses and lavender fill the air with scent. The herb garden grows culinary and medicinal plants. I returned in July to the butterfly garden, where monarchs and swallowtails fed on nectar. The Scented Woodland Walk offers a shaded path lined with dogwood and spicebush, releasing soft aromas when you brush past leaves.

Workshops run year-round. I took a flower-arranging class that provided branches and early blooms. The instructor shared tips on trimming stems and changing water. Other workshops cover composting, beekeeping, and native plant propagation.

The Children's Garden is a hands-on space where kids dig, water, and observe insects under magnifiers. On a Saturday visit, schoolchildren built scarecrows for a fall festival— laughter and chatter filled the air.

The Tea Garden Café overlooks a small pond. It serves sandwiches, soup, and hot drinks. One afternoon, I sipped mint tea grown on-site while watching dragonflies skim the water. The café accepts credit cards and offers vegetarian and gluten-free options.

Photography is popular. Early morning light is best for flower shots, and tripods are allowed on weekdays. I once arrived at 7 AM to capture dew on iris petals with no one else around.

In winter, the garden hosts "Garden Lights," a display of LED installations among trees and sculptures from late November through January. I bundled up with friends and wandered winding paths illuminated in color. Tickets are CA$20 and include hot chocolate.

Restrooms are in the main building. Parking is free for two hours; after that, a small fee applies. Bus 34 runs every 10 minutes from Lawrence Station.

Urban Birdwatching & Wildlife

Locations to Explore:

- **Tommy Thompson Park (Leslie Spit):** 1 Leslie St, Toronto, ON M5A 1S3

- **High Park:** 1873 Bloor St W, Toronto, ON M6R 2Z3

- **Don Valley Trails:** See above section.
  Price: Free; guided walks CA$5–10 per person.
  Activities/Things to Do: Birdwatching, wildlife photography, guided nature tours, nature journaling.
  How to Get There:

- **Tommy Thompson Park:** 15-minute bike ride or taxi from downtown; limited parking onsite.

- **High Park:** Subway Line 2 to High Park Station.

- **Don Valley Trails:** As above.
  Best Time to Visit:

- **Spring Migration (April–May):** Peak warbler and songbird diversity.

- **Fall Migration (September–October):** Raptors and shorebirds passing through.
  Why You Should Visit: Toronto's green spaces host a surprising range of birds and wildlife—easy to reach and free to explore.
  Additional Info:

- Bring binoculars and a field guide or bird ID app (Merlin, eBird).

- Respect wildlife—keep distance and stay on trails.
- Check Toronto Field Naturalists for guided walk schedules.

City parks double as wildlife corridors. At Tommy Thompson Park, a man-made spit into Lake Ontario, shorebirds and waterfowl stop during migration. On a May morning, I biked out onto the breakwater and saw sandpipers and plovers probing the sand. A local birder pointed out a ruddy turnstone, its orange legs flashing in the sun.

High Park's woodlands attract warblers, woodpeckers, and chickadees. I joined a guided bird walk in late April and stood quietly under maples while a yellow-rumped warbler flicked through branches. The leader taught us to listen for calls and watch for wing flashes. After the walk, I borrowed a guidebook from a fellow birder and spent another hour spotting downy woodpeckers.

In the Don Valley, look for raptors. I once heard a barred owl hoot at dusk along the trail. Using a flashlight, I located it perched high in an oak—its eyes reflecting back like amber gems. That same evening, a red-tailed hawk circled overhead, scanning for rodents.

Tommy Thompson Park is also good for migrant waterfowl in spring and fall. Paths can be muddy—wear waterproof boots. Parking is limited; arriving by bike or taxi avoids the hassle.

Guided walks by Toronto Field Naturalists and other groups run weekly from April through October. They're led by experienced birders who share tips on identifying calls and plumage. Fees are around CA$5, and walks last two hours. I've attended Humber Bay Park walks, spotting gulls, terns, and even a pelican flying low over the water.

For self-guided trips, use an app like Merlin Bird ID. It can identify birds by song or photo. Carry a notebook to record species and behaviors.

Wildlife sightings aren't limited to birds. In ravines and river trails, look for turtles, frogs, and small mammals. On a summer afternoon along the Humber River Trail, I watched a painted turtle sun itself on a log and a family of mallard ducks glide by.

Always stay on marked trails and keep dogs on leash. Wildlife can be stressed by off-trail noise. During nesting season (May–July), extra care is needed.

Chapter 9: Day Trips from Toronto

Niagara Falls

Niagara Falls is one of the world's most spectacular natural wonders, sitting about 90 minutes southwest of Toronto. It's actually made up of three falls—Horseshoe Falls, American Falls, and Bridal Veil Falls—but the sweeping curve of Horseshoe Falls on the Canadian side is the showstopper. When you stand at Table Rock, you'll feel the ground tremble under your feet and hear the roar of millions of gallons of water crashing below. This mix of raw power and easy access makes Niagara Falls a perfect day trip.

Address:
Queen Victoria Park, Niagara Falls, ON L2E 3E4

Price:

- **Falls View:** Free.

- **Hornblower Niagara Cruises:** CAD 35 /adult, CAD 25 /child (6–12).

- **Journey Behind the Falls:** CAD 23 /adult, CAD 16 /child.

- **Skylon Tower Observation Deck:** CAD 20 /adult, CAD 14 /child.

- **Floral Showhouse:** CAD 5 /person.

Activities & Things to Do:

- **Hornblower Cruise:** Board at Table Rock and glide into the mist. Ponchos are provided but expect to get wet.

- **Journey Behind the Falls:** Take an elevator down 125 feet into tunnels behind Horseshoe Falls. Observation portals let you hear and feel the water's power.

- **Clifton Hill:** If you're traveling with family or want a carnival vibe, this strip has arcades, mini-golf, the Movieland Wax Museum, and a giant Ferris wheel.

- **Skylon Tower:** Ride the glass-front elevator up 775 feet for 360° views of the falls, Niagara River, and Toronto skyline on clear days. The revolving restaurant is a bonus.

- **Niagara Parkway:** Rent a bike or walk along this 35 km route. Stop at the Butterfly Conservatory (CAD 17 /adult) or Queen Victoria Park's flower gardens.

- **Falls Illumination & Fireworks:** From dusk until midnight, colored lights illuminate the falls. In summer, weekend fireworks add extra sparkle.

How to Get There:

- **By Car:** Take the QEW west from Toronto. Exit at Niagara Falls and follow signs to Queen Victoria Park. Parking is CAD 10–15/day.

- **By GO Train & Bus:** From Union Station, take a GO train to Burlington, then transfer to a GO bus to Niagara Falls. Total time ~2.5 hrs; round-trip ~CAD 30.

- **By Direct Bus:** Megabus and Greyhound run direct routes from Toronto Coach Terminal; tickets from CAD 25 round-trip.

Best Time to Visit:

- **Late May–Early October:** All attractions open, weather 15–25 °C.

- **Summer Weekdays:** Fewer crowds than weekends.

- **Spring (Apr–May):** Peak water flow from snowmelt; some attractions open later.

- **Fall (Sep–Oct):** Cooler air, colorful foliage, smaller crowds.

Why You Should Visit:

Niagara Falls is a bucket-list destination for its sheer power and beauty. It's one of the few natural wonders you can approach so closely without a long hike. Beyond the falls, you'll find botanical gardens, historic sites, and a range of dining options. Whether you're chasing adrenaline on the Hornblower, soaking up the view from Skylon Tower, or simply strolling the park, there's something for every traveler.

Additional Info & Tips:

- **Border Crossing:** To visit the U.S. side, bring a passport and check Peace Bridge wait times.

- **Dress for the Mist:** A waterproof jacket or poncho and quick-dry clothes keep you comfortable.

- **Accessibility:** Most viewpoints, boats, and elevators are wheelchair accessible.

- **Family-Friendly:** Picnic areas at Dufferin Islands, a playground in Queen Victoria Park, and family washrooms at Table Rock Centre.

- **Crowds:** Peak summer (July–August) is busy—arrive before 10 am or after 4 pm to beat the lines.

- **Food & Drink:** On-site restaurants can be pricey; pack snacks to save time and money.

Personal Anecdote: I once timed my visit for the summer fireworks series. As the first burst of light exploded over the falls, the mist caught the colors, casting rainbows everywhere. It felt like nature's own light show—an unforgettable moment.

Niagara-on-the-Lake (Wineries & Historic Town)

Just 20 minutes north of Niagara Falls, Niagara-on-the-Lake is often called Ontario's prettiest town. With tree-lined streets, Victorian architecture, and boutique wineries, it feels like stepping into a living postcard. Whether you're a wine lover, history buff, or theatergoer, this compact town delivers a relaxing day trip.

Address:
Old Town Niagara-on-the-Lake, ON L0S 1J0

Price:

- **Wine Tastings:** CAD 12–18/person (premium flights up to CAD 25).
- **Shaw Festival:** CAD 30–100+/ticket, depending on show and seating.
- **Fort George:** CAD 12 /adult, CAD 8 /student or senior.
- **Bike Rental:** CAD 25/day.
- **Carriage Tour:** CAD 15–20/person for 30 minutes.

Activities & Things to Do:

- **Winery Hopping:** Home to 20+ wineries, including Peller Estates for classic flights and Inniskillin for world-famous ice wine. Many offer vineyard tours and food pairings.
- **Shaw Festival:** April–October, staging works by Shaw, Shakespeare, and modern playwrights. Multiple venues around town.
- **Fort George:** A restored War of 1812 fort with musket demonstrations, costumed interpreters, and a small museum.

- **Biking the Lakeshore:** Rent a bike and pedal along Lake Ontario's shore. Picnic stops, orchards, and small beaches line the route.

- **Carriage & River Tours:** Horse-drawn carriages wind through historic streets; river cruises on the Niagara River offer a different view of the town.

- **Spa Treatments:** Several day spas use grape-based products—book a wine-infused massage or body wrap for a unique treat.

How to Get There:

- **By Car:** QEW east from Niagara Falls, exit 37 to Niagara-on-the-Lake. Municipal parking lots charge CAD 2–4/hour.

- **By Bus:** Niagara-on-the-Lake Transit shuttles hourly from Niagara Falls and St. Catharines for CAD 3/ride.

- **Guided Tours:** Many operators in Toronto and Niagara Falls offer full-day packages with transport, winery stops, and a walking tour.

Best Time to Visit:

- **June–September:** Warm weather, open patios, full winery schedules.

- **October:** Harvest events, fall colors, grape stomps.

- **December:** Christmas market and festive lights.

- **May:** Magnolia and cherry blossoms line Queen Street.

Why You Should Visit:

Niagara-on-the-Lake blends small-town charm with world-class wine and theater. Sip award-winning vintages in a sunlit tasting room, catch a play at the Festival Theatre, then stroll boutique-lined Queen Street. It's a peaceful counterpoint to Niagara Falls' energy.

Additional Info & Tips:

- **Book Ahead:** Shaw Festival and popular winery tours fill up quickly on weekends.
- **Shop Hours:** Many boutiques and tasting rooms close by 5 pm on Sundays.
- **Dining:** Afternoon tea at the Prince of Wales Hotel is a treat; Balzac's Café is great for coffee and pastries.
- **Etiquette:** Tip your winery guide and avoid strong perfumes that interfere with wine aromas.
- **Walking Shoes:** Cobblestone streets make comfortable shoes a must.

Personal Anecdote: I once stumbled upon an impromptu jazz trio playing in a winery courtyard. With a glass of Riesling in hand and the warm sun overhead, it felt like a private concert among the vines.

Blue Mountain & Collingwood

About two hours north of Toronto, Blue Mountain Resort and nearby Collingwood offer a mix of outdoor thrills and small-town charm. In winter, you can ski or snowboard on 43 runs; in summer, the Ridge Runner Mountain Coaster and TreeTop Trekking ziplines deliver adrenaline. Collingwood's waterfront, shops, and craft breweries add a laid-back vibe to round out your day.

Address:
Blue Mountain Resort, 190 Gord Canning Dr, The Blue Mountains, ON L9Y 0V4
Downtown Collingwood, Hurontario St & Ste Marie St, Collingwood, ON L9Y 1A1

Price:

- **Winter Day Pass:** CAD 100–150/adult (season and day dependent).

- **Mountain Coaster:** CAD 25/ride; combo (coaster + zipline) ~CAD 60.
- **TreeTop Trekking:** CAD 35–45/course.
- **Bike Rental:** CAD 30/day.
- **Heritage Walking Tour:** CAD 15/person.

Activities & Things to Do:

- **Skiing & Snowboarding:** 43 runs for all levels, plus night skiing. On-site rental shops make gear easy.
- **Ridge Runner Coaster:** Control your speed down a forest track—slow for views or speed up for thrills.
- **TreeTop Trekking:** Navigate suspension bridges and ziplines above the forest canopy with trained guides.
- **Hiking & Biking:** Trails range from easy lakeside paths to challenging climbs with panoramic Georgian Bay views.
- **Collingwood Beach:** Swim, sunbathe, or picnic on sandy shores with a view of the bay.
- **Downtown Collingwood:** Explore boutiques, coffee shops, and craft breweries like Sawdust City Brewing Co.
- **Seasonal Events:** Summer music festivals, farmers' markets, and holiday markets in winter.

How to Get There:

- **By Car:** Hwy 400 north to Hwy 26 west; about two hours from Toronto.
- **By Bus:** GO Transit and shuttle services run seasonally; tickets ~CAD 40 round-trip.
- **By Train:** Train to Barrie, then bus or rideshare—less direct but possible.

Best Time to Visit:

- **Winter (Dec–Mar):** Peak ski season; weekdays are quieter.

- **Summer (Jun–Aug):** Warm days for coaster rides and beach time.
- **Fall (Sep–Oct):** Harvest festivals and fall foliage.
- **Shoulder Seasons:** Limited activities; check resort calendar.

Why You Should Visit:
Blue Mountain is Ontario's top all-season resort, combining adrenaline-pumping activities with lakeside relaxation. You can ski or zipline in the morning, then unwind with a craft beer on a sunny patio overlooking Georgian Bay. Rentals and lessons on-site make it easy, even if you arrive without gear.

Additional Info & Tips:
- **Gear Rentals & Lessons:** Book lessons in advance; rental shops often get busy on weekends.
- **Parking:** CAD 20/day at the resort; free parking in Collingwood with shuttle service.
- **Crowds:** Weekends and holidays are busiest—midweek trips mean shorter lift lines.
- **Dining:** The Blue Mountain Village has casual and upscale options; in Collingwood, try The Tremont Cafe for breakfast and Side Launch Brewing for beer.
- **Overnight Option:** Stay in a Collingwood B&B to extend your trip.

Practical Tip: On my last visit, I hit the Ridge Runner first thing, then biked the trails, and ended with a lakeside picnic on Collingwood Beach. A full day of adventure without feeling rushed.

Prince Edward County

Often called "Ontario's Hamptons," Prince Edward County is a laid-back peninsula about three hours east of Toronto. It's known for sandy beaches, rolling vineyards, and a vibrant arts scene. Spend your day lounging on freshwater dunes, tasting local wines, and browsing galleries in towns like Picton and Wellington.

Address:
Picton Main Street, Picton, ON K0K 2T0 (central hub)

Price:

- **Sandbanks Park Day Pass:** CAD 17/vehicle (up to 7 people).
- **Wine Tastings:** CAD 10–20/person.
- **Art Gallery Admissions:** CAD 5–10.
- **Bike Rental:** CAD 30/day.
- **Kayak/Canoe Rental:** CAD 25–40/hour.

Activities & Things to Do:

- **Sandbanks Provincial Park:** Home to some of the world's largest freshwater sand dunes. Swim, sunbathe, or hike the dunes and wooded trails. Picnic tables and washrooms on site.
- **Winery Tours:** Over 40 wineries, including Norman Hardie for Riesling, Sandbanks Winery for lakefront tastings, and Hinterland for bold reds. Many offer vineyard tours and barrel tastings.
- **Art & Culture:** Visit Oeno Gallery in Bloomfield or Red Barn Gallery near Wellington. Street murals and artist studios dot the countryside.

- **Farmers' Markets:** Seasonal markets in Picton and Wellington (May–Oct) with produce, baked goods, cheeses, and crafts.
- **Water Activities:** Kayak or canoe around Sandbanks or Hay Bay Marsh.
- **Cycling:** Quiet county roads link beaches, wineries, and farm stands—ideal for a leisurely bike tour.

How to Get There:
- **By Car:** Hwy 401 east, exit onto County Rd 49 south, follow signs to Picton—about 3 hrs from Toronto.
- **By Bus:** Daily services to Picton from Toronto via Coach Canada.
- **By Train & Taxi:** VIA Rail to Belleville, then a 30-minute taxi or rideshare to the County.

Best Time to Visit:
- **Summer (Jun–Sep):** Beach weather and open winery patios.
- **Fall (Sep–Oct):** Harvest events, fall foliage, and grape stomps.
- **Spring (May):** Fewer crowds, early blooms in gardens and orchards.
- **Winter:** Many businesses closed, though some wineries host cozy tastings.

Why You Should Visit:
Prince Edward County offers beach time, wine country, and artsy small towns in one trip. Swim in the morning, taste Riesling in the afternoon, and catch an outdoor concert at the Regent Theatre in Picton by evening. It's a place that encourages slowing down and enjoying simple pleasures.

Additional Info & Tips:

- **Book Early:** Sandbanks campsites and popular B&Bs fill up by spring for summer dates.

- **Cash & Cards:** Most wineries take cards, but smaller stands may prefer cash.

- **Dining Reservations:** Weekend crowds make booking ahead wise.

- **Respect Private Property:** Stay on designated paths at vineyards and farms.

- **Sun Protection:** Dunes reflect sunlight—bring sunscreen and a hat.

Real-Life Example: One July, I spent the morning swimming at Sandbanks, biked to Norman Hardie for a Riesling tasting, then ended the day watching a concert at the Regent Theatre. It was the perfect blend of nature, wine, and culture.

Hamilton Waterfalls Tour

Just an hour from Toronto, Hamilton is nicknamed the "City of Waterfalls" with over 100 cascades scattered around the city. You can hit several in one day, each offering a different character—from towering drops to gentle streams. A Hamilton waterfalls tour is ideal for hikers, photographers, and families wanting an easy nature escape.

Address:

- **Spencer Gorge (Webster's & Tews Falls):** 905 York Road, Dundas, ON L9H 5E4

- **Albion Falls:** 310 Upper Gage Avenue, Hamilton, ON L8W 3N9

- **Devil's Punchbowl:** 1160 Centennial Parkway North, Hamilton, ON L8E 2R9

Price:

- **Park Access:** Free; some lots charge CAD 2–5/visit.
- **Guided Tours:** CAD 25–40/person for waterfall hikes.
- **Dundas Peak Parking:** CAD 2/hour.

Activities & Things to Do:

- **Webster's & Tews Falls:** In Spencer Gorge, these twin falls drop 22 m and 41 m. Well-marked trails lead to viewpoints above and below the falls.
- **Albion Falls:** A 19 m tiered falls near the Red Hill Valley Parkway. A short walk from the lot brings you to a stone viewing platform.
- **Dundas Peak:** A 30-minute hike rewards you with sweeping views of the gorge and Lower City. You might see paragliders launching on windy days.
- **Devil's Punchbowl:** A bowl-shaped falls with a boardwalk and staircase for easy viewing.
- **Lower City Falls:** Smaller cascades like Felker's, Borer's, and Westcliffe Falls are within a short drive of each other.
- **Photography:** Early morning or late afternoon light highlights the water's movement. Waterproof boots let you shoot from the falls' base.
- **Picnicking & Birdwatching:** Many parks have tables and benches. Look for herons and kingfishers along the riverbanks.

How to Get There:

- **By Car:** Take the QEW or Hwy 403 from Toronto to Hamilton. Follow signs to Dundas or Stoney Creek for specific falls.
- **By GO Train & Bus:** GO train to Aldershot Station, then local bus or rideshare to trailheads.

- **Guided Hikes:** Local outfitters offer pickup from downtown Hamilton.

Best Time to Visit:

- **Spring (Apr–May):** Snowmelt creates peak flows—falls are at their fullest.

- **Summer (Jun–Aug):** Trails dry out, long daylight hours.

- **Fall (Sep–Oct):** Cooler air, fall colors along the gorges.

- **Winter:** Check trail closures—frozen falls are beautiful but only for experienced hikers with proper gear.

Why You Should Visit:

Hamilton's waterfalls tour offers backcountry feel with minimal travel. You don't need to drive hours into the wilderness—many falls are a short hike from parking lots. It's perfect for a quick nature fix close to the city.

Additional Info & Tips:

- **Trail Conditions:** After rain, paths get muddy and slippery. Wear sturdy, grippy footwear.

- **Safety:** Stay on marked trails and behind railings. Rocks near falls can be slick.

- **Pack Water & Snacks:** Facilities are limited—bring your own refreshments.

- **Respect Nature:** Carry out trash, stay on trails, and avoid disturbing wildlife.

- **Timing:** Plan your route in advance if you want to hit multiple falls—start early to make the most of daylight.

Practical Tip: I mapped a morning route that hit Webster's Falls, then Albion Falls, and ended at Devil's Punchbowl for lunch by the water. Short drives and easy hikes made it feel like a waterfall safari without rushing.

Stratford (Shakespeare Festival)

About two hours southwest of Toronto, Stratford is a riverside town famous for the Stratford Festival—one of North America's top theater events. The town itself is easy to explore on foot, with Victorian-era buildings, a scenic riverwalk, and cozy cafés. A Stratford day trip combines culture, history, and small-town charm.

Address:
Stratford Festival Theatre, 55 Queen Street, Stratford, ON N5A 6V2

Price:

- **Festival Tickets:** CAD 30–100+ per show.
- **Guided Walking Tours:** CAD 10–15 for 90 minutes.
- **Avon River Cruise:** CAD 12 /adult, CAD 8 /child.
- **Stratford Perth Museum:** CAD 8 /adult, CAD 5 /child.

Activities & Things to Do:

- **Stratford Festival:** April–October, featuring Shakespeare, Shaw, and modern plays. Multiple venues host full-scale productions and intimate studio shows.
- **Avon River:** Rent a paddleboat or join a narrated river cruise to learn about Stratford's history and see swans gliding by.
- **Downtown Stroll:** Queen Street's galleries, boutiques, and cafés are perfect for browsing. Don't miss Why Not Chocolates for handmade truffles.
- **Stratford Perth Museum:** Housed in a former jail, it covers local history, including the festival's origins.
- **Festival Theatre Gardens:** Landscaped gardens behind the main theater offer a peaceful break between shows.

- **Farmers' Market:** Saturdays (May–Oct), with fresh produce, baked goods, and crafts.

How to Get There:

- **By VIA Rail:** Direct trains from Union Station take about 2 hours; fares start at CAD 40 one-way.
- **By Car:** Hwy 401 west to Exit 275 (Perth County), then follow signs to Stratford. Parking in municipal lots is CAD 1.50/hour.
- **By Bus:** Daily service from Toronto via Greyhound or Coach Canada.

Best Time to Visit:

- **April–October:** Festival season with full show schedules.
- **June–August:** Outdoor concerts and warmer weather.
- **Fall (Sep–Oct):** Crisp air, fall foliage, fewer crowds.
- **Winter:** Limited shows and closed gardens—check the festival calendar.

Why You Should Visit:

Stratford offers a rare blend of world-class theater and small-town beauty. Even if you skip the shows, the river, Victorian architecture, and laid-back cafés make for a pleasant stroll. A matinée followed by a riverside lunch is a day well spent.

Additional Info & Tips:

- **Show Times:** Matinée and evening performances allow you to see two shows in one day—plan meal breaks accordingly.
- **Dining Reservations:** Restaurants near the theater fill up on show nights—reserve ahead.
- **Walking Shoes:** Sidewalks can be uneven; comfortable shoes help.

- **Free Performances:** Look for pop-up music and street performers in parks.
- **Accessibility:** Most venues and attractions are wheelchair accessible; contact box office for assistance.

Personal Anecdote: On a cool May afternoon, I saw "Much Ado About Nothing" in the Avon Theatre. Afterward, I wandered the riverbank and found a harpist playing under a willow tree—it felt like the arts were everywhere you turned.

St. Jacobs & Mennonite Country

An hour-and-a-half west of Toronto, St. Jacobs & Mennonite Country offers a glimpse into traditional Mennonite life, a bustling farmers' market, and peaceful countryside. It's a chance to slow down, taste farm-fresh foods, and shop for handcrafted goods.

Address:
St. Jacobs Farmers' Market, 878 Weber St N, Waterloo, ON N2J 4A7

Price:
- **Market Entry:** Free.
- **Guided Farm Tours:** CAD 15–20/person for 2 hours.
- **Mennonite Village Museum:** CAD 8 /adult, CAD 5 /child.
- **Bike Rental:** CAD 30/day.

Activities & Things to Do:
- **Farmers' Market:** Open Tuesdays and Saturdays year-round, with 200+ vendors selling produce, meats, cheeses, baked goods, crafts, and antiques. Don't miss the maple syrup and cheese stalls.
- **Mennonite Village Museum:** Explore original homesteads, a blacksmith shop, and costumed interpreters demonstrating traditional crafts.

- **Country Tours:** Bus or buggy tours explain Mennonite farming practices, traditions, and community life.
- **Cycling & Hiking:** Quiet backroads link farms and fields—stop at roadside stands for fresh fruit or homemade pies.
- **Antique & Artisan Shops:** St. Jacobs village is known for its antique malls, woodworking shops, and quilt stores.
- **Railway Museum:** In nearby Elmira, see historic locomotives and rail artifacts (CAD 5/person).

How to Get There:

- **By Car:** Hwy 401 west to Waterloo exit, then county roads to St. Jacobs. Free parking at the market.
- **By GO Train:** Train to Kitchener, then taxi or rideshare to St. Jacobs.
- **Guided Tours:** Toronto-based tour companies offer full-day trips with transport, market visits, and museum stops.

Best Time to Visit:

- **May–October:** Farmers' market, farm tours, and good cycling weather.
- **December:** Special Christmas market with decorations, live music, and holiday treats.
- **Winter:** Fewer tours run; check availability.

Why You Should Visit:

St. Jacobs & Mennonite Country is an immersive cultural escape close to the city. You can fill your basket with farm-fresh eggs, local honey, and hand-stitched quilts, then step into a horse-drawn buggy or wander through historic farmhouses. It's a lesson in simplicity, craftsmanship, and community.

Additional Info & Tips:

- **Cash Preferred:** Many vendors accept cash only. ATMs on site can have long lines on Saturdays.

- **Photography Etiquette:** Ask before photographing people in traditional dress.

- **Peak Hours:** Saturdays 9 am–noon are busiest; Tuesdays are quieter.

- **Food & Drink:** Sample homemade sausages, pies, and apple cider. Small cafés and bakeries nearby offer lunch options.

- **Facilities:** Public washrooms are near the market entrance and in the village centre.

Real-Life Example: One spring Tuesday, I cycled from Kitchener to St. Jacobs on quiet backroads, stopped at a farm stand for strawberries, then spent the afternoon browsing antique shops. It felt like discovering a hidden corner of Ontario that moves at its own pace.

Chapter 10: Family-Friendly Activities

Toronto Zoo

Toronto Zoo is one of the largest zoos in the world, spread over 710 acres and divided into regions like Africa, the Americas, Indo-Malaya, and the Tundra. It's a full-day adventure, with over 4,000 animals to see. I still remember the look on my niece's face when a polar bear swam right past the underwater viewing tunnel—she squealed and pressed her hands against the glass. Whether you're into big cats, primates, or birds, there's something to captivate every age.

Address, Price & How to Get There
2000 Meadowvale Rd, Toronto, ON M1B 5K7. Admission is Adults $29, Children (3–12) $19, and under 3 enter free. From downtown, take the TTC Line 2 to Kennedy Station, then transfer to Bus 86A (Meadowvale) or Bus 12A (Kingston Rd). The bus drops you right at the main entrance. If you drive, there's paid parking on-site.

Activities & Things to Do
Walk through the African Savanna to spot giraffes and zebras grazing side by side. In the Tundra Trek, you'll find polar bears and Arctic foxes in realistic icy habitats; watch the bears dive under water through glass panels. The Kids' Zoo has a petting area where little ones can feed goats and sheep. In summer, head to Splash Island—an outdoor water play zone with tunnels and sprinklers that cool you off after a long walk.

Best Time to Visit & Why
Late spring through early fall offers full exhibit access and active animals. Weekdays are quieter, especially in the morning

when animals are most active. If you come during shoulder season (May or September), you'll avoid crowds and still enjoy pleasant weather. Early mornings are ideal for seeing big cats prowling and bears exploring before it gets too warm.

Why You Should Visit

Toronto Zoo combines education with entertainment. Interactive keeper talks and scheduled feedings let you learn about conservation and animal behavior. The layout is stroller-friendly and has plenty of shaded rest areas. If you have kids who love animals—or even reluctant animal-lovers—they'll come away with new favorite species and big smiles.

Additional Info & Tips

Stroller rentals and wheelchairs are available at the main entrance. There are several food courts offering kid-friendly meals, plus picnic areas if you bring your own. Download the zoo's map app to plan your route and check feeding times. Washrooms are well-marked, and water bottle refill stations are scattered throughout.

Personal Anecdote & Final Thoughts

On a sunny June morning, my family arrived right when the zoo opened. By lunchtime, we'd seen elephants, orangutans, and even caught a keeper feeding the snow leopards. My niece declared it "the best day ever," and we still joke about the time she tried to race a cheetah in the Kids' Zone—no contest, of course. If you want a mix of education, excitement, and pure joy, Toronto Zoo is a can't-miss.

Ontario Science Centre

The Ontario Science Centre turns curiosity into play. With hands-on exhibits, a planetarium, and an IMAX Dome, it's perfect for kids who ask "why?" at every turn. I once took my nephew, who's obsessed with space, and watching his eyes light up in the planetarium as stars zoomed past was priceless. It's where science feels like a playground, and adults often learn a thing or two themselves.

Address, Price & How to Get There
770 Don Mills Rd, North York, ON M3C 1T3. Admission is Adults $22, Youth (3–17) $13, and under 3 free. From Pape Station on the Bloor–Danforth line, catch TTC Bus 25 (Don Mills) straight to the front entrance. If you drive, there's free parking in the lot.

Activities & Things to Do
Explore the Weston Family Innovation Centre, where you can build circuits, experiment with robotics, and test your own designs. The Science Arcade offers retro games powered by simple machines. Don't miss the KidSpark zone, tailored for under-8s with water tables, giant bubbles, and climbing structures. In the afternoon, head to the planetarium for "Northern Skies," a show that turns the dome into a night sky filled with constellations.

Best Time to Visit & Why
Weekday mornings during the school year are the least crowded—ideal if your kids get overwhelmed by noise. Arrive right at opening to beat the lines for the IMAX Dome and planetarium. Summer weekends fill up fast, so if you must come then, aim for a late-afternoon session when many families start to leave.

Why You Should Visit
The Centre blends fun and learning seamlessly. Kids are encouraged to touch, press, and experiment—there's no "don't touch" sign in sight. Exhibits rotate regularly, so even if you've been before, you'll find something new. Plus, the IMAX Dome's giant screen and surround sound make science documentaries feel epic.

Additional Info & Tips
Pack snacks or plan to eat at the cafeteria; the menu has sandwiches, salads, and kid-friendly options. There are quiet

zones and seating areas for breaks. Lockers near the entrance keep your belongings safe while you explore. Don't forget to check the daily schedule for special demos and workshops.

Personal Anecdote & Final Thoughts

My nephew still talks about the time he made a mini-robot arm and used it to pick up blocks. He beamed with pride when I video-called his parents to show off his creation. The Ontario Science Centre isn't just a museum—it's a place where kids build confidence along with their experiments. It's hands-down one of my favorite spots for a family outing in Toronto.

LEGOLAND Discovery Centre Toronto

If your kids live and breathe LEGO, this indoor playground is heaven. Located in Vaughan Mills Mall, it's smaller than the big parks but packed with rides, build zones, and a 4D cinema. When my cousin's twins visited, they spent hours constructing cars and racing them down the launch ramp—then begged to go back the next day.

Address, Price & How to Get There

1 Bass Pro Mills Dr, Vaughan, ON L4K 5W4. Admission is about $30 per person; check online for seasonal deals and combo tickets with nearby attractions. From Toronto, take York Region Transit routes 77 or 96 to Vaughan Mills Mall, or drive and use the mall's free parking.

Activities & Things to Do

Ride the Kingdom Quest Laser Ride and zap trolls alongside knights. In the 4D cinema, watch short films with wind, mist, and light effects that bring LEGO stories to life. The Build & Test Zone challenges you to build cars or planes and see which design goes fastest. Don't miss MINILAND Toronto—a miniature cityscape made entirely of LEGO, complete with moving trains and working lights.

Best Time to Visit & Why
Weekday mornings are the quietest, especially right after opening. Weekends can get busy, so if your schedule allows, visit Tuesday–Thursday. During school breaks, check for early-bird or late-afternoon discounts—many families prefer midday, so those slots tend to be calmer.

Why You Should Visit
It's a perfect rain-or-cold-day activity since it's fully indoors. The mix of rides, creative play, and impressive LEGO models appeals to a wide age range (3–12). Staff members are patient and helpful, offering building tips and keeping the play zones organized. Plus, it's a fun way for parents to unleash their inner child.

Additional Info & Tips
Children under 16 must be accompanied by an adult, and adults need a child's ticket. Bring socks—some play areas require them. If you plan to shop at Vaughan Mills, look for combo deals that include LEGOLAND and the mall's outlets. There's a small café inside, but you can also grab a meal in the food court.

Personal Anecdote & Final Thoughts
When the twins built a four-wheeled "monster truck," they insisted on racing it against every other creation in the zone. The staff even gave them a little "champion" sticker for their design. LEGOLAND Discovery Centre may be compact, but the excitement it sparks can fill a whole day—and create memories that last much longer.

Toronto Islands (Centreville & Splash Pad)

Just a 15-minute ferry ride from downtown, Toronto Islands feel like a world apart. Centre Island's amusement park, petting zoo, and water play area make it a top pick for families. I spent an afternoon here with friends, and watching our kids pedal quadricycles along tree-lined paths while the skyline shimmered across the water was pure magic.

Address, Price & How to Get There
Ferries depart from Jack Layton Ferry Terminal at 9 Queens Quay W. Round-trip fares are Adults $9.11, Children (2–14) $4.29, under 2 free. Ferries run every 15–30 minutes; buy tickets online or at the terminal. On arrival, follow signs to Centreville Amusement Park and the nearby Splash Pad.

Activities & Things to Do
Centreville offers 30+ rides geared toward young children— think gentle carousels, miniature trains, and the classic Ferris wheel. The petting zoo lets kids feed goats and sheep under staff supervision. Splash Pad has water jets, tunnels, and dumping buckets for cooling off. You can also rent bikes, kayaks, or paddle boats to explore further afield on the quieter islands.

Best Time to Visit & Why
Late spring through early fall is peak season—ride all the attractions and enjoy water play. Weekday visits avoid long ferry lines, and arriving at the first ferry (around 9:00 AM) gives you several uncrowded hours. Late afternoons are quieter too, as many families head home by 4:00 PM.

Why You Should Visit
It's a car-free environment where kids can run safely, and parents can relax under shady trees. The mix of rides and free play lets families tailor their day. Plus, the skyline views across Lake Ontario are unbeatable—perfect for a family photo with Toronto's towers in the background.

Additional Info & Tips
Pack a picnic lunch or snacks; food on the islands can be pricey and limited in healthy options. Bring sunscreen, hats, and insect repellent. There are washrooms near Centreville and at the Splash Pad. Lockers are available for rent if you want to store towels or extra clothes.

Personal Anecdote & Final Thoughts

On a warm July day, my friends and I packed sandwiches and rode the ferry at 8:45 AM. We snagged a picnic table under a maple tree, then hit the rides before the crowds arrived. By midday, our kids were squealing in the Splash Pad while we watched with coffee in hand. A day on the islands feels like a mini-vacation—and it's only minutes from the city.

Hockey Hall of Fame

Even if you're not a hockey fanatic, the Hockey Hall of Fame delivers a fun, interactive experience. Located in the historic Bank of Montreal building, it's where you can touch the Stanley Cup and test your skills in goalie simulations. I took my nephew there on a rainy afternoon, and he spent half an hour trying to stop virtual slapshots—he still talks about it weeks later.

Address, Price & How to Get There

30 Yonge St, Toronto, ON M5E 1X8. Admission is Adults $25, Youth (4–13) $15, under 4 free. A short five-minute walk from Union Station (TTC Lines 1 & 2), or you can catch any streetcar to King Street and walk east.

Activities & Things to Do

Pose with the real Stanley Cup and snap photos in the trophy gallery. In the NHLPA Zone, you can test your shot speed and accuracy against a simulated Carey Price. The multimedia timeline traces hockey's evolution from pond games to pro leagues. Don't miss the Life Size statues of legends like Wayne Gretzky and Bobby Orr for great photo ops.

Best Time to Visit & Why

Any day of the year works since it's fully indoors, but weekday afternoons are quieter. Arrive when it opens to explore the main exhibits before guided tour groups arrive. If there's an off-season NHL lockout or break, fan traffic dips—perfect for strolling through at your own pace.

Why You Should Visit
It's a uniquely Canadian experience that mixes sport, history, and technology. Kids love the hands-on simulations, and adults appreciate the memorabilia. The building itself has beautiful marble interiors and historic vaults that once stored gold—another neat aspect to explore.

Additional Info & Tips
There's a small café on-site serving coffee, snacks, and sandwiches. The gift shop carries jerseys, pucks, and team souvenirs. If you plan to ride the Go Train to nearby attractions, Union Station's connectivity makes combining visits easy.

Personal Anecdote & Final Thoughts
After my nephew finally scored on the goalie simulation, he jumped up and down with pride, and we bought a little souvenir puck to remember the moment. Even if you don't skate or follow hockey, the energy and history here are infectious. It's a fun way to dive into Canada's national sports.

Riverdale Farm

Riverdale Farm is a surprising slice of countryside tucked into the city's east end. It's a working farm with cows, pigs, goats, and chickens—all free to visit. I once took my daughter on a crisp October morning and she couldn't stop naming every animal she saw. It's peaceful, educational, and a perfect break from busy city streets.

Address, Price & How to Get There
201 Winchester St, Toronto, ON M4X 1B8. Admission is free. Take the 506 Carlton streetcar to Winchester Street and walk south for two blocks, or get off at Castle Frank Station (Line 2) and walk east along the footpath.

Activities & Things to Do
Stroll through the barns to watch farmers feed piglets and groom sheep. The outdoor pens let you get close to goats—some are friendly enough for a gentle pet. There's a vegetable

garden, orchard, and historic farmhouse to explore. On weekends, you might catch a volunteer-led demonstration on milking or wool spinning.

Best Time to Visit & Why
Spring and fall are ideal—baby animals appear in spring, and fall brings colorful leaves and harvest festivals. Summer can be hot, so mornings are best for animal activity. Winter visits offer a quiet, snowy landscape but fewer animals outdoors.

Why You Should Visit
It's one of the few free, working farms in a major city. Kids learn where food comes from and can connect with animals in a hands-on way. Parents appreciate the open space and picnic tables under mature trees.

Additional Info & Tips
Pack a snack or lunch; there are picnic spots near the pond. Wear sturdy shoes—some paths can be muddy. Bring a camera for adorable animal photos. Washrooms are available in the main barn.

Personal Anecdote & Final Thoughts
On my daughter's fifth birthday, we surprised her with a visit. She spent an hour chasing chickens (under supervision) and giggling at piglets squealing for food. Riverdale Farm is a simple pleasure, but it's moments like those that make family trips special—and it won't cost you a dime.

Children's Museums & Libraries

Toronto's libraries and kid-focused museums offer hours of free or low-cost fun. From storytime sessions to interactive exhibits, they're great for rainy days or budget-friendly outings. My friend's son still talks about building paper rockets at a library STEM workshop—it sparked his love of science.

Addresses, Prices & How to Get There

- **Lillian H. Smith Branch, TPL:** 239 College St, Toronto, ON M5T 1R5. Free admission. Take TTC Line 1 to College Station, then walk west.

- **Bata Shoe Museum:** 327 Bloor St W, Toronto, ON M5S 1W7. Adults $14, Youth (6–18) $10, under 6 free. A short walk from St. George Station.

- **TIFF Kids digiPlaySpace:** Housed in TIFF Bell Lightbox, 350 King St W, ON M5V 3X5. Ticketed exhibit, check website for prices. Walk from King Station.

Activities & Things to Do

At Lillian H. Smith, join free daily storytimes, puppet shows, and craft sessions. The children's floor is full of colorful reading nooks and interactive literacy games. At the Bata Shoe Museum, family weekends feature hands-on workshops where kids design their own paper shoes. digiPlaySpace blends digital media with physical play—kids code simple animations, remix film clips, and collaborate on giant video walls.

Best Time to Visit & Why

Library events run year-round; check the TPL events calendar for morning storytimes (10–11 AM) when attendance is lower. Museum family days often happen on weekends; arrive at opening to avoid crowds. Summer camps and drop-in workshops fill up fast, so book in advance.

Why You Should Visit

These spots are designed for children's engagement and learning. They're affordable (or free), well-staffed, and offer structured and unstructured play. Libraries foster early literacy, while museums spark creativity and curiosity in themed exhibits.

Additional Info & Tips

Get a free Toronto Public Library card for access to digital resources, museum passes, and book loans. Bata offers family membership deals that include guest passes. Bring socks for digiPlaySpace—some areas require them. Check each venue's website for special events, holiday closures, and booking requirements.

Personal Anecdote & Final Thoughts

One rainy afternoon, my friend and I took her son to a TPL coding workshop. He proudly built a simple video game in 45 minutes and couldn't wait to show his parents. Whether it's storytime magic or a hands-on museum exhibit, Toronto's children's venues deliver learning disguised as fun. They're perfect go-to spots when you need a break from the sun or the budget.

Chapter 11: Festivals, Events & Seasonal Fun

Toronto International Film Festival (TIFF)

Date: Early September (10 days, usually first or second week)

Every September, Toronto turns into a global film capital when TIFF rolls into town. For ten days, venues across the city—from the sleek TIFF Bell Lightbox downtown to the grand Roy Thomson Hall—host premieres, special screenings, and filmmaker talks. If you love movies, this festival is your playground.

Activities & Things to Do:

- **Screenings:** Catch big-budget premieres, thought-provoking documentaries, and indie darlings. Many films debut here before heading to theaters.

- **Red-Carpet Events:** If you score a gala pass, you can walk the red carpet or watch stars arrive. Even without a pass, you can hang near the entrance to spot a celebrity or two.

- **Workshops & Panels:** Filmmakers and actors often stick around for Q&A sessions. I once stayed after a screening of a Canadian short film to hear the director explain her inspiration—and ended up chatting about her hometown over coffee.

- **Street Style Watching:** King Street West becoTmes a runway of street fashion. Grab a coffee, find a bench, and watch the buzz.

Why Attend: TIFF isn't just for industry insiders. As an everyday visitor, you get access to films months before they hit cinemas. I queued up at dawn for a midnight screening of a breakout Canadian feature and ended up swapping theories with local cinephiles until 2 AM. It's a chance to meet fellow film fans, discover new directors, and soak in the electric atmosphere.

Practical Tips & Additional Info:

- **Passes & Tickets:** Single "rush" tickets go on sale at 9 AM daily for around $20–$30 CAD. Festival passes cost more but include guaranteed seats and priority access. Plan and buy online as soon as dates are announced.

- **Getting Around:** Most venues sit along King Street West between John and Bathurst. The 504 King streetcar runs frequently, or you can walk if you're staying downtown.

- **Apps & Planning:** Download the TIFF app for screening times, venue maps, and real-time seat availability. Build your schedule early; popular films sell out fast.

- **Comfort & Gear:** Wear comfy shoes—you'll walk between venues. Carry a refillable water bottle and small snacks, since concession lines can be long.

Caribana (Toronto Caribbean Carnival)

Date: Late July–Early August (Grand Parade on first weekend of August)

Caribana is Toronto's summer street party, a ten-day celebration of Caribbean music, food, and culture. When I first joined the Grand Parade, I didn't know what to expect—but by the end of the day I was drenched in paint, dancing to soca beats, and grinning ear to ear.

Activities & Things to Do:

- **Grand Parade:** Watch or join costumed masqueraders as they march down Lakeshore Boulevard with vibrant floats and loud music.

- **J'ouvert Morning:** The unofficial festival kickoff happens before dawn. Revelers cover themselves in colored paint and powder while DJs spin steelpan and soca tracks.

- **Junior Carnival:** A scaled-down parade for families and kids, with prizes for best costumes.

- **Food Fair:** Sample jerk chicken, doubles, roti, and other Caribbean specialties from dozens of food stalls.

Why Attend: Caribana is about more than bright costumes—it's about community and joy. One August, I joined the crowd at J'ouvert, and by sunrise I'd danced with strangers who felt like old friends. You'll taste authentic Caribbean dishes, learn dance moves, and experience the island spirit in Toronto.

Practical Tips & Additional Info:

- **Cost:** Grand Parade viewing is free. Special events like the King & Queen Show cost around $30–$50 CAD.

- **Best Viewing Spots:** Arrive early along Lakeshore between Cherry Beach and Ontario Place for clear views. Bring a small chair or blanket if you plan to sit.

- **Transit:** The parade route is closed to cars. Use the 501 Queen streetcar to Broadview, then switch to a shuttle bus to the Lakeshore.

- **What to Wear:** Light, breathable clothes you don't mind staining during J'ouvert. Pack sunscreen, sunglasses, and a hat.

- **Safety:** Keep valuables in a zip-lock bag. Stay hydrated— local vendors often sell water bottles.

Winterlicious & Summerlicious

Date:

- **Winterlicious:** Late January–Early February (2 weeks)
- **Summerlicious:** Mid-July (2 weeks)

Twice a year, Toronto's restaurant scene goes on sale. For two weeks, over 200 eateries offer set three-course menus at special prices. Whether you're craving sushi, French bistro fare, or plant-based delights, there's a deal waiting.

Activities & Things to Do:

- **Prix-Fixe Menus:** Enjoy three courses—appetizer, main, dessert—at fixed rates: Lunch $23–33 CAD, Dinner $33–53 CAD.
- **Chef Demos & Tastings:** Some restaurants host live cooking demos or wine pairings. It's a chance to meet chefs and learn kitchen tips.
- **Neighborhood Food Tours:** Guided walks through Little Italy, Chinatown, and Leslieville stop at several participating spots.

Why Attend: I once snagged a $33 Winterlicious lunch at a high-end French restaurant that normally charges $60 for the same meal. I felt like a VIP as I sampled duck confit and macarons without breaking the bank. It's the perfect excuse to try a restaurant you've eyed for months.

Practical Tips & Additional Info:

- **Reservations:** Book early—some spots fill up within hours of reservations opening. Use the official Dine.TO site or call restaurants directly.
- **Dietary Restrictions:** Many menus note vegetarian, vegan, and gluten-free options. If you have allergies, call ahead.

- **Menu Previews:** Check restaurant websites for sample menus. That way you know you're getting dishes you'll love.

- **Timing:** For quieter service, aim for early lunch or midweek dinners.

Nuit Blanche

Date: First Saturday in October (sunset to sunrise)

For one night each October, Toronto becomes a city-wide art gallery. From dusk until dawn, you can wander streets, parks, and buildings transformed by light installations, performance art, and interactive exhibits.

Activities & Things to Do:

- **Art Installations:** Discover sculptures that glow, projections on historic façades, and sound-activated pieces in public spaces.

- **Pop-Up Performances:** Catch dance troupes, spoken-word artists, and musicians in unexpected spots—from subway platforms to parking lots.

- **Guided Tours:** Join a free walking tour focused on Indigenous art, architecture, or technology in contemporary installations.

Why Attend: Nuit Blanche is one of those events you have to experience to believe. I remember stumbling on a mirrored maze under the Gardiner Expressway that reflected city lights into hundreds of angles—it felt like stepping into another world. You'll meet fellow night owls, share headphones for audio pieces, and rediscover familiar streets.

Practical Tips & Additional Info:

- **Maps & App:** Download the official Nuit Blanche map or app to plan your route. Exhibits spread across Queen West, the Distillery District, and the waterfront.

- **Getting Around:** TTC runs 24-hour service on major lines. If you prefer cycling, Toronto's bike-share stations stay open all night.

- **What to Bring:** Dress in layers—October nights can be chilly. Pack snacks, a water bottle, and a power bank for your phone.

- **Safety:** Stick to well-lit areas, travel in pairs if possible, and keep your belongings secure.

Canadian National Exhibition (CNE)

Date: Mid-August through Labour Day (about 18 days)

Known simply as "The Ex," the CNE is Toronto's summer tradition. Held on Exhibition Place grounds, it blends a county fair with a showcase of Ontario's agriculture, food, and entertainment.

Activities & Things to Do:

- **Midway Rides & Games:** Test your courage on roller coasters and try your luck at ring toss or balloon darts.

- **Agricultural Exhibits:** See prize-winning livestock, giant pumpkins, and flower competitions.

- **Live Entertainment:** From big-name concerts on the Bandshell stage to circus acts in the Coliseum.

- **Food Pavilion:** Sample mini-donuts, deep-fried everything, and unique treats like poutine fries.

Why Attend: Visiting the CNE feels like stepping into a time machine. One summer evening, I held a turkey leg in one hand and watched a motorcycle stunt show in the other—there was something timeless about the bright lights and carnival music. It's a chance to try weird foods, cheer on farm animals, and enjoy shows that you won't see anywhere else.

Practical Tips & Additional Info:

- **Admission:** General gate admission is around $20 CAD. Save by buying advance tickets online or using a CNE pass if you plan multiple visits.

- **Getting There:** Take the Exhibition GO train or the TTC Exhibition Loop. Parking is limited and expensive.

- **Money Tips:** Bring cash for midway games and food vendors; ATMs charge fees.

- **Best Time to Go:** Weekdays are less crowded. If you want to see big concerts, check the schedule in advance.

Pride Toronto

Date: June (Pride Parade on last weekend)

Each June, Toronto bursts into rainbow colors for Pride. The highlight is the parade down Church Street, but the celebration stretches across the month with events for every taste.

Activities & Things to Do:

- **Pride Parade:** Floats, performers, and marchers flood Yonge and Bloor, heading down Church Street. Join in or watch from the sidelines.

- **Dyke March & Trans March:** Community-focused events leading up to the main parade.

- **Pride Village:** A street festival with live music, food trucks, vendor stalls, and a beer garden.

- **Nightlife:** Special club nights, rooftop pool parties, and drag brunches.

Why Attend: Pride Toronto is more than a party—it's a statement of inclusion and rights. I'll never forget standing under a rainbow flag with thousands of people, singing along to a drag queen's set. It felt like being part of something bigger than myself, united in celebration.

Practical Tips & Additional Info:

- **Cost:** Most events are free. Nightclub parties usually charge $20–$60 CAD at the door.
- **Location:** Church and Wellesley is the heart of Pride Village. It's easy to reach via Bloor-Yonge subway station.
- **Safety & Comfort:** Bring water, wear sunscreen, and plan meeting points with friends in case you get separated.

Toronto Christmas Market & Winter Activities

Date: Late November–December 23 (Christmas Market); November–March (skating)

When winter arrives, Toronto transforms into a holiday wonderland. The Distillery District Christmas Market brings Old World charm, while ice rinks and light displays pop up across the city.

Activities & Things to Do:

- **Christmas Market:** Browse wooden chalets selling crafts, ornaments, and warm treats like mulled wine and German sausages.
- **Ice Skating:** Glide under the city lights at Nathan Phillips Square rink or the Bloor-Yorkville rink.
- **Light Displays:** Wander the Distillery District's fairy-lit lanes and snap photos by the giant Christmas tree.
- **Carriage Rides & Hot Chocolate Tours:** Cozy up on a horse-drawn carriage or join a guided tour with stops for steaming cocoa.

Why Attend: I first visited the Distillery District market on a snowy evening and felt transported to a European village. The scent of pine and spice filled the air as I sipped glühwein under twinkling lights. It's the perfect spot for a date night or family outing—magical without leaving Toronto.

Practical Tips & Additional Info:

- **Market Admission:** Around $6–8 CAD; the first hour each day is free. Arrive early to beat the crowds.

- **Skate Rentals:** Cost about $10 CAD. If you bring your own skates, you skate free.

- **Dress for Cold:** Wear layers, waterproof gloves, a warm hat, and insulated boots—the wind off Lake Ontario can be harsh.

- **Transit & Parking:** Take the 504 King streetcar or the 514 Cherry streetcar to the Distillery District. Parking is limited and pricey.

Chapter 12: Sample Itineraries

One-Day in Toronto: Highlights Sprint

Overview & Timing:
If you have just 24 hours in Toronto, you can still cover the city's signature sights without feeling too rushed. Plan to start around 8 am and finish by 8 pm. You'll spend roughly $60–$100 CAD per person on admission fees and lunch, plus any extras like coffee or souvenirs. Wear comfortable shoes and dress in layers—Toronto's weather can shift from cool mornings to warm afternoons. I once tackled this route on a spring Saturday: by pacing myself and arriving early, I skipped most lines and even squeezed in a mid-day gelato break.

Morning at CN Tower & Ripley's Aquarium:
Begin at the CN Tower (290 Bremner Blvd). Aim to arrive by 8 am to beat the crowds. A LookOut Level ticket is $38 CAD; if you crave an adrenaline rush, the EdgeWalk is $225 CAD (includes safety briefing and harness) and lasts about 90 minutes. From Union Station, it's a quick 5-minute walk via the SkyWalk. After soaking in the 360° view—on a clear day you can see across Lake Ontario—head next door to Ripley's Aquarium (288 Bremner Blvd). Admission is $42 CAD. Plan about 90 minutes to wander through the moving sidewalk tunnel under sharks and rays. Don't miss the jellyfish gallery—the shifting pastel lights feel almost meditative.

Midday at St. Lawrence Market:
Walk east along Front Street for about 12 minutes, or hop on the 509 streetcar at Queens Quay. At St. Lawrence Market

(93 Front St E), budget $15–$25 CAD for lunch. Carousel Bakery's peameal bacon sandwich ($6.50 CAD) is a local legend—grab one to go and find a bench in the south wing. I once waited in line chatting with a vendor who shared stories about the market's history dating back to 1803. After eating, wander the stalls: you'll find Quebec cheeses, fresh oysters, artisanal bread, and global street eats. Public restrooms and water fountains are available on the upper level.

Afternoon in the Distillery District:
From the market, take the 504 King streetcar west to Trinity Street. The Distillery Historic District (Trinity St & Mill St) is free to enter. Spend an hour exploring Victorian brick buildings turned art galleries and boutiques. At Spirit of York Distillery, tasting flights start at $15 CAD if you want to sample small-batch gin. On weekends, check the courtyard for pop-up artisan fairs—on one visit, I learned basic pottery techniques from a local ceramist. The cobblestone lanes and restored warehouses make for great photos.

Evening at Harbourfront & Dinner:
Catch the 509 streetcar back to Queens Quay West and head to Harbourfront Centre (235 Queens Quay W). You can rent a kayak for $20 CAD/hour or join a free lakeside walking tour. Sunset here is magical—the light shimmers on the water and the city skyline glows. For dinner, try Icebreaker Fish & Chips (207 Queen's Quay W) where a plate runs $18–$25 CAD. The haddock is flaky, and the hand-cut fries come with malt vinegar. Afterward, stroll toward Canada Place under street lamps. Pro tip: download the TTC app beforehand to track streetcar arrivals so you're never left guessing

Weekend Getaway: Balanced Mix

Overview & Budget:
With two days in Toronto, you'll sample the city's urban buzz and a touch of lakeside calm. Expect to spend about $200–$300 CAD per person (excluding lodging). A downtown hotel

near King or Queen Station saves transit time, letting you pack in more experiences. I tried this on a May weekend—waking up steps from the action meant I could grab an early coffee and head out before crowds arrived.

Day 1 Morning: Kensington Market & Chinatown:
Start at Kensington Market (Kensington Ave & Nassau St) around 9 am. It's free to explore, though budget $10 CAD for a latte at Moonbean Café (91 Kensington Ave). Take the subway to Spadina Station, then walk north on Kensington Ave. Browse vintage shops, artisanal bakeries, and bold murals—don't miss the hidden alley near Augusta Ave, where new street art appears overnight. By late morning, head two blocks south into Chinatown on Spadina Ave. Grab dim sum at Rol San (323 Spadina Ave), with plates running $5–$10. I once learned dumpling-folding tips from the owner, which made the meal feel extra special.

Day 1 Afternoon & Evening:
Around 1 pm, catch the 510 streetcar west to Queen Street West. Stroll between Spadina and Portland to find indie boutiques and Graffiti Alley (Queen St W between Spadina & Portland). Spend about 45 minutes snapping photos. By 4 pm, take the streetcar to Queen & Ossington and walk north along the Ossington Strip (Ossington Ave between Queen & Dundas). Sample craft beer at Bellwoods Brewery (124 Ossington Ave) for $8 per pint. For dinner, reserve at Bar Raval (505 College St) for Spanish tapas—small plates $10–$18. Their patatas bravas are a must. I once shared a sangria pitcher with friends there and ended up dancing to live music nearby.

Day 2 Morning: Toronto Islands:
On Saturday morning, head to Jack Layton Ferry Terminal (9 Bay St). Round-trip tickets are $8.19 CAD; buy online to skip lines. Ferries depart every 15–30 minutes. At Centre Island, rent a bike for $8 CAD/hour and cycle past Centreville Amusement Park and sandy beaches. The view back at Toronto's skyline is

unbeatable. Pack a picnic or grab ice cream at the snack stand. I love relaxing at Hanlan's Point and watching sailboats drift by.

Day 2 Afternoon & Dinner:
Return by 2 pm and stroll west along Queens Quay to Harbourfront Centre (235 Queens Quay W). The Power Plant Contemporary Art Gallery is free, and the plaza often hosts markets or live music. Spend an hour exploring. For dinner, take the 509 streetcar to Byblos (11 Wellington St E) for Eastern Mediterranean fare—$25–$40 CAD per person. Their grilled lamb and flatbreads stand out. Book ahead; weekend tables fill fast. End with gelato from Dolce Gelato (10 Queens Quay W) and a leisurely lakeside walk back.

5-Day Cultural Deep Dive

Overview & Focus:
Art lovers and history buffs will feel at home on this five-day tour of Toronto's cultural landmarks. Plan for $600–$800 CAD per person (admissions and meals). I did this in October, when cooler weather made museum-hopping comfortable and the fall colors added extra charm to outdoor sculpture gardens.

Day 1: Museum Mile
Begin at the Royal Ontario Museum (100 Queens Park). Admission is $23 CAD. Take the subway to Museum Station. Allow 2–3 hours to explore dinosaurs, ancient Egypt, and the modern Michael Lee-Chin Crystal. After lunch at the ROM café ($15–$20 CAD), walk next door to the Gardiner Museum (111 Queens Park). Entry is $16 CAD. Its ceramics collection ranges from ancient pottery to contemporary pieces. If you're curious, join a 30-minute pottery demo for about $5 CAD extra.

Day 2: Art Gallery of Ontario & Graffiti Alley
Visit the Art Gallery of Ontario (317 Dundas St W). Admission is $25 CAD, but it's free Wednesday evenings after 6 pm. Take the subway to St Patrick Station and walk west. Spend 2–3 hours on Group of Seven landscapes and modern exhibits. I'll

never forget seeing Lawren Harris's snowy scenes up close. In the afternoon, stroll through Graffiti Alley (Queen St W between Spadina & Portland). It's free, and the murals change regularly—perfect for photos.

Day 3: Indigenous & Cultural Centres
Head to the Native Canadian Centre of Toronto (16 Spadina Rd) by subway to Spadina Station. Entry is donation-based. On weekends, join a drumming circle—I once took part and felt the strong community spirit. After lunch ($12–$18 CAD), take the 192 bus from St George Station to the Aga Khan Museum (77 Bloor St E). Admission is $18 CAD. Its Islamic art and serene gardens offer a peaceful afternoon.

Day 4: Film & Theatre
Experience Toronto's film scene at TIFF Bell Lightbox (350 King St W). Screening tickets run $15–$20 CAD. Take the subway to King Station. After a morning indie film, stroll to the Royal Alexandra Theatre (260 King St W) for an evening play. Tickets start at $30 CAD. The historic venue dates to 1907 and adds a classic touch to any performance.

Day 5: Literary & Music Scene
Spend your final day in Leslieville at Type Books (883 Queen St E). Browse new releases ($15–$25 CAD/book) over coffee. In the afternoon, head to the Toronto Music Garden (479 Queens Quay W). It's free, and guided tours run May–October; otherwise, wander the paths inspired by Bach's music. Finish with live jazz at The Rex (194 Queen St W). There's usually a $10 cover, and drinks are $8–$12. Their late-night shows run until 2 am.

Foodie's Itinerary: Tasting Your Way Through TO

Overview & Costs:

Toronto's culinary scene is a true melting pot. In one full day, budget $150–$250 CAD per person for meals and snacks. You'll visit markets, street-food stalls, cafés, and sit-down restaurants. I did this in late spring—booking brunch spots ahead and wearing comfortable clothes helped me move smoothly from one flavor to the next.

Breakfast & Mid-Morning Snack:

Begin at St. Lawrence Market (93 Front St E) at 8 am. A peameal bacon sandwich from Carousel Bakery costs $6.50 CAD, and a coffee at the market café is about $3. Take the subway to King Station, then walk five minutes. After breakfast, explore stalls selling cheese, olives, and fresh pastries. Around 10 am, head to Kensington Market via Spadina Station and grab a vegan empanada at Seven Lives Tacos (68 Kensington Ave) for $4 CAD. The kick of spices wakes you right up.

Lunch:

By noon, walk two blocks south into Chinatown for dumplings at Mother's Dumplings (421 Spadina Ave). A plate of pork and chive dumplings plus soup costs about $10 CAD. It's busy at lunch, so go early or after 1 pm. I once arrived at 11:45 am and skipped the line entirely. The simple setup and communal tables make it easy to chat with locals about other hidden eats.

Afternoon Coffee & Gelato:

After lunch, take the 504 streetcar east to the Distillery Historic District. Stop at Balzac's Coffee Roastery (1 Tank House Lane) for a $5 latte and seasonal pastry—try the almond croissant if it's available. Spend some time browsing galleries and boutiques. If it's warm, grab gelato at Brick Street Bakery ($4 per scoop) and stroll the cobblestone lanes. I once discovered salted honeycomb flavor by chance—it's now my go-to.

Dinner & Late-Night Bite:
For dinner, reserve at Pai (18 Elizabeth St), near Queen Station. Their Northern Thai dishes—like khao soi—are $10–$18 CAD. The décor is casual, and you can adjust the spice level. Don't skip the mango sticky rice for dessert. Afterward, walk north to Poutini's House of Poutine (111 Spadina Ave) for a classic poutine ($9 CAD). It's the perfect late-night treat: hot gravy, cheese curds, and hand-cut fries. If you're still peckish, they offer chicken and vegan poutine too.

Family Trip: Kid-Friendly & Interactive

Overview & Budget:
Toronto has plenty of hands-on fun for families. Over one full day (or two), budget $120–$200 CAD per person for admissions and meals, plus $10–$20 CAD for transit and ferry. I tested this with my niece and nephew last summer, and balancing indoor science exhibits with outdoor play kept them engaged all day.

Morning at the Ontario Science Centre:
Start at the Ontario Science Centre (770 Don Mills Rd). Admission is $22 CAD per adult and $16 CAD per child (ages 3–12). From Eglinton Station, take the 25 Don Mills bus (about 20 minutes). Inside, interactive exhibits like the rainforest hall and space gallery can fill 2–3 hours. Don't miss the live science show at 11 am. My niece loved the earthquake simulator, and my nephew couldn't get enough of the pulleys demonstration. The on-site café serves sandwiches and snacks for $8–$12 CAD.

Lunch at Evergreen Brick Works:
After the Science Centre, catch the 28 Bayview bus from Broadview Station to Evergreen Brick Works (550 Bayview Ave). Café Orso on-site offers flatbreads ($12–

$15 CAD) and hot chocolate ($4). The grounds include walking trails and a small pond where ducks gather—feed them birdseed from the café for $2. On weekends, a farmers' market sells fresh fruit and baked goods. I'll never forget my niece's delight feeding ducks for the first time.

Afternoon at the Toronto Zoo:
Next, take the 85 Sheppard East bus from Don Mills Station to the Toronto Zoo (2000 Meadowvale Rd). Admission is $29 CAD per adult and $19 CAD per child. The zoo spans 287 hectares, so focus on highlights: the African savanna exhibit with giraffes and zebras, and the splash pad near Kid's Zoo for cooling off. The panda exhibit requires a special ticket ($10 extra). Plan to spend 2–3 hours here. On busy days, use the zoo's shuttle train to move between zones.

Late Afternoon & Dinner:
In the late afternoon, head back downtown for Centreville Amusement Park on Toronto Islands. Take a taxi or rideshare to Jack Layton Ferry Terminal (9 Bay St) and catch the ferry ($8.19 CAD round-trip). Centreville wristbands are $20 CAD per person for unlimited rides. The carousel, Ferris wheel, and mini-roller coaster are perfect for younger kids. After the ferry ride back, walk east along Queens Quay to The Old Spaghetti Factory (54 The Esplanade). Pasta plates cost $15–$20 CAD, with smaller kids' portions available. The vintage décor and twinkling lights make for a cozy family dinner. My nephew still talks about the stained-glass lamps above our table.

Outdoorsy Traveler: Green Toronto in 3 Days

Overview & Costs:
Toronto surprises with green spaces close to downtown. Over three days, budget $80–$150 CAD per person for transit, rentals, and parking. Pack a refillable water bottle, sturdy shoes,

and layers. I did this in early fall—when leaves turned orange and red, every trail felt like a postcard.

Day 1: High Park & Grenadier Pond:

Take the subway to High Park Station. Entry is free. In spring, the cherry blossoms along West Road draw crowds—plan to arrive by 8 am for photos. You can rent a bike at Parkside Rentals (1875 Bloor St W) for about $10 CAD/hour. Cycle the park's paved paths, stopping at Grenadier Pond for a picnic. Trails wind through wooded areas where you might spot wild turkeys or peacocks near the animal garden. There are public washrooms near the main entrance and picnic tables by the pond.

Day 2: Scarborough Bluffs & Bluffer's Park:

On day two, head east. From Kennedy Station, take the 12 Kingston Rd bus to Brimley Rd, then walk to Bluffer's Park (1 Brimley Rd S). Parking is $10 CAD if you drive; otherwise, transit is free. Hike the Waterfront Trail for sweeping views of Lake Ontario from 60-meter-high cliffs. Bring sunscreen and water—the sun reflects off the water and can feel intense. After hiking, cool off by dipping your toes in the lake. If you need a snack, the marina concession sells fish and chips for $8–$12 CAD.

Day 3: Don Valley Trails & Evergreen Brick Works:

For the final day, take the 28 Bayview bus from Broadview Station to Evergreen Brick Works (550 Bayview Ave). Entry and parking are free. The Don Valley trail system stretches for kilometers—ideal for hiking, trail running, or mountain biking. I joined a weekend trail-run group at 9 am; they set a relaxed pace and welcomed newcomers. After your workout, explore the Brick Works site—a reclaimed quarry turned environmental hub. On weekends, a farmers' market offers coffee ($4 CAD) and local produce.

Gear & Practical Tips:

- **Transit & Parking:** Use the TTC app for schedules. For parking, try the Go Parking app.
- **Rentals:** Reserve bikes or kayaks online when possible.
- **Safety:** Trails can be slippery after rain—wear grippy shoes and carry a small first-aid kit.
- **Food & Water:** Pack snacks and water; concessions are limited.
- **Timing:** Weekdays and early mornings are quieter. I found that starting before 9 am gave me peaceful trails and better wildlife sightings.
These three days reveal Toronto's green side—an unexpected mix of urban and wild.

Romantic Escape: Date Spots & Scenic Views

Overview & Budget:
For a memorable date, blend free and splurge experiences with a budget of $120–$200 CAD per couple. Start in the afternoon and linger late into the night. I surprised my partner with this route last summer, and the mix of relaxed spots and a special dinner made it unforgettable.

Afternoon at Sugar Beach:
Head to Sugar Beach (11 Dockside Dr) around 3 pm. It's free and easy to reach: take the 509 streetcar to Queen's Quay East, then walk south. The small sandy area with pink umbrellas feels like a private retreat. Pack a picnic blanket and snacks from a nearby market. I once set up a cheese board here, and fellow beachgoers asked where we found our grapes. The gentle breeze off Lake Ontario is perfect for sitting close together.

Early Evening at 360 Restaurant:
As sunset approaches, walk to the CN Tower

(290 Bremner Blvd). A prix-fixe dinner at 360 Restaurant costs about $75 CAD per person and includes LookOut Level admission. From Union Station, it's a five-minute walk through the SkyWalk. Reserve a window table so you can watch the city rotate beneath you—the dining room completes a full circle in 72 minutes. Pair your meal with Ontario wines; the lamb entrée is a favorite. The combination of gourmet food and panoramic views feels truly special.

Nightcap at Polson Pier:
After dinner, head to Polson Pier (11 Polson St) by taxi or rideshare (about $10 CAD). At Cabana Pool Bar on the rooftop, cocktails run $12–$15 CAD. The night view of Toronto's skyline reflecting on the water is breathtaking. Bring a light jacket—the lake breeze can be chilly. I once toasted with a cocktail named "Northern Lights" while city lights danced across the water—it felt like our own private world.

Tips & Extras:

- **Timing:** Book dinner around 7 pm to catch sunset. Check online for seasonal sunset times.

- **Reservations:** Both 360 Restaurant and Cabana Pool Bar fill up quickly—reserve at least a week ahead.

- **Dress Code:** Smart casual is perfect.

- **Photos:** For Sugar Beach, use a phone tripod or ask a friendly passerby for a couple shot under the pink umbrellas.

- **Sweet Finish:** If you want one more treat, stop by SOMA Chocolatemaker (16 Bridgman Ave) for a shared dessert before heading back.
  This blend of free relaxation and one splurge spot makes for a day that's both intimate and unforgettable—a true Toronto date

CONCLUSION

As you close this guide and turn your thoughts toward packing your bags, remember that Toronto isn't just a list of sights—it's a living, breathing city ready to surprise you at every turn. From the soaring heights of the CN Tower to the hidden murals in Graffiti Alley, you've seen how every neighborhood has its own story. Whether you're sampling poutine at a street cart or catching a show at a local theatre, Toronto welcomes you to write your own adventure. This city thrives on curiosity, so lean in, ask questions, and let yourself get a little lost now and then.

No matter how many tips you carry, the best memories often come from unplanned detours. If you stumble upon a pop-up market in Kensington or hear a busker on Queen Street, pause and join the crowd. Talk to the artist, try a new dish, or simply sit and watch the city go by. These small moments—sharing a laugh with a shop owner, swapping stories with a fellow traveler—are what turn good trips into great ones. Keep your mind open and your schedule flexible, and you'll discover the side of Toronto that most guidebooks never mention.

To make the most of your time, here are a few practical pointers: pick up a Presto card for easy access to buses, streetcars, and subways; pack layers, because lake breezes can turn a sunny day into a chilly one; and wear comfortable shoes—you'll be walking more than you think. Budget a little extra for that unexpected concert ticket or the perfect souvenir you can't resist. And if you're here in winter or summer, check local event calendars— Toronto's festivals and markets are as much a part of the city's spirit as its skyline.

Above all, remember that travel is about connection. Toronto's strength lies in its people—the friendly barista who remembers your name, the gallery owner who shares a hidden artist, the neighborly wave on a bike path. Embrace those connections, and you'll leave with more than photos; you'll carry new friendships and fresh perspectives home with you. So go ahead—step out, say hello, and let Toronto show you what makes it one of the world's most welcoming cities. Safe travels, and may your journey be as vibrant and varied as the city itself.